Oriental Asia:
Themes Toward a Geography

PRENTICE-HALL

Foundations of World Regional Geography

PHILLIP BACON *and* LORRIN KENNAMER, *Editors*

Foundations of World Regional Geography

Oriental Asia

Asia

THEMES TOWARD
A GEOGRAPHY

Joseph E. Spencer

University of California

PRENTICE-HALL, INC., Englewood Cliffs, New Jersey

Library of Congress Cataloging in Publication Data

SPENCER, JOSEPH EARLE.
   Oriental Asia: themes toward a geography.

   (Foundations of world regional geography series)
   Bibliography: p.
   1.   Asia—Description and travel.   I.   Title.
DS10.S63   915   73–5645
ISBN 0–13–642843–6
ISBN 0–13–642835–5 (pbk.)

Printed in the United States of America
10 9 8 7 6 5 4 3 2 1

PRENTICE-HALL INTERNATIONAL, INC., *London*
PRENTICE-HALL OF AUSTRALIA, PTY. LTD., *Sydney*
PRENTICE-HALL OF CANADA, LTD., *Toronto*
PRENTICE-HALL OF INDIA PRIVATE LIMITED, *New Delhi*
PRENTICE-HALL OF JAPAN, INC., *Tokyo*

Contents

Figures

CHAPTER 1 the sub-continental setting

The Orient is at once ancient, middle-aged, and young; it is convoluted, complex, and simple; it is mysterious, unfathomable, and straightforward. It all depends on that facet of the Orient one is trying to examine, the time perspective employed, and who is doing the examining. To the American tourist catching glimpses of ancient Hindu rites at a festival of historic origin, the Orient may well be mysterious and unfathomable; to an occidental political scientist watching contemporary parliamentary maneuvers of Philippine congressmen in Manila, the pattern may well appear convoluted; to a Taiwan Chinese industrialist seeking a new site for a manufacturing plant at which to produce goods for the American market, the Orient is new but full of opportunity. To the geographer who takes the long view of the Orient, this part of the world appears as a multiple set of mixed patterns, with many overlapping subsystems, varied environments, and contrasting historical outlooks framed into a single mosaic.

There are conventions in the systems of reference to southern and eastern Asia, but these often are academic conventions, and no great heed is paid them here. The Orient properly comprises the southeastern "fourth" of the great continent of Eurasia, and it can be conceived as Southeast Asia in the broadest sense, the same sense in which Europe is the northwestern sector of the great continent, the USSR the northern sector, and in which the southwestern sector forms part of the Islamic World (Fig. 1, inset). There is, of course, another and more restricted usage of the term Southeast Asia that refers to the *very* southeastern unit of the continental mainland, Burma, Thailand, Laos, Cambodia, Vietnam, Malaysia, Indonesia, and the Philippines, in a context in which the Far East signifies China, Korea, and Japan, and in which Southern Asia now signifies India, Pakistan, Bangladesh, and Ceylon. This one convention is recog-

politicocultural components
of the oriental world

1

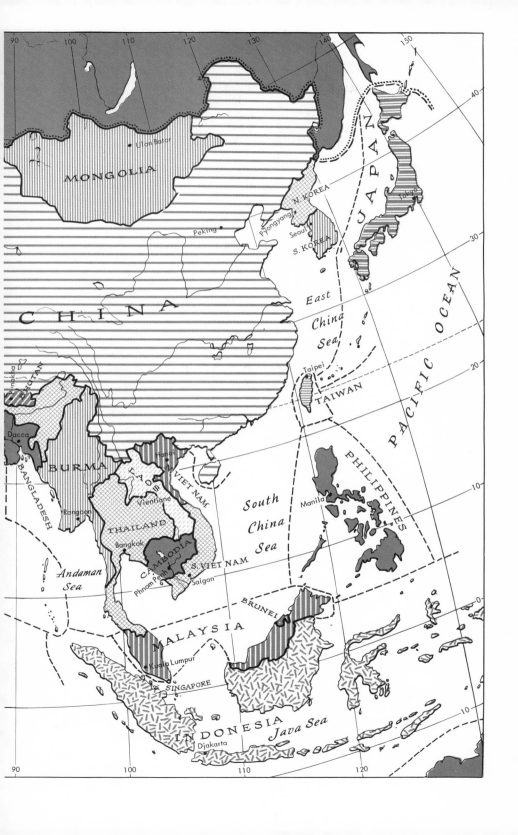

nized in this volume, and the terms the Orient, Oriental Asia, and the Oriental world will be employed in the broad reference to all those lands lying between Pakistan, eastern Indonesia, and northern Japan. Numerous other conventions will be ignored in aspects of regional reference, since this small volume attempts a widely ranging coverage of a complex set of conditions in rather practical terms.

As the southeastern sector of Eurasia, the Orient is, in the physical sense, a rather motley assemblage of mountainous highlands, assorted high basins and plateaus, riverine and coastal lowlands, appended marginal peninsulas, and intricate offshore island chains. In the human sense the Orient is the home of about half the world's population, involving many different racial strains and a huge number of languages, clothing costumes, and dietary systems. In the economic sense Oriental Asia comprises a most mixed lot of economies, from industrialized Japan to agricultural Ceylon, most of the territory having strong local and regional contrasts in economy. In the political sense the Orient is a battleground for most of the ideas devised by man as to how societies should be organized and administered. In social terms the Orient is not only the home of several of the earth's great religions and systems of philosophy, but it is also the home region for some of the earth's most restrictive codes of daily performance. In cultural terms Oriental Asia includes two great culture systems, the Indian and the Chinese, each of which has its regional adherents in the sense that Ceylon belongs to the Indian realm and Japan to the Chinese realm (Fig. 1). There are also numerous smaller sub systems, some of which predate either the Indian and Chinese systems, and some of which are generically related but variant systems having their own intrinsic features. The two major, regional systems have historically overlapped in spatial terms and are in cultural conflict in the peninsular sector of Southeast Asia in what constitutes a cultural shatter belt. But the Orient has also been disturbed by intrusive elements from the outside, as by the world of Islam and the world of the Occident, most expressive in Pakistan and in the Philippines. And so it goes, for one can list many other elements in the mosaic.

There is one other convention that this volume must obey, the editorial discretion by which one author is required to deal, in one volume, with an inordinately large region, half the earth's population, and the most complex of all its sets of cultural systems, while another author may cope with but a corner of the earth. Necessarily, then, coverage in this volume must be brief, normal regional discussion omitted, and many subjects left untreated. This little volume needs to be viewed as "essays on the geography of the Oriental world" and not as a "summary of the geography of the Orient."

The Orient in Physical Structure

The Orient begins on the roof of the Eurasian continent, in the Tibetan highland and the plateaus of Mongolia, but its most significant pieces lie strewn around the southern and eastern margins of the continent in a series of stepped-down units that form great peninsulas, massive lowland blocks, great river valleys, and arclike festoons of islands lying offshore (Fig. 2). As we look at these, figuratively, from a mountain perch in the Tibetan highland, we find ourselves on an eastern segment of the great folded and faulted mountain system that extends across Eurasia from Spain to Burma. The Tibetan section of this great system is the tallest and most massive of all, containing the world's tallest mountains in Everest, Kanchenjunga, and other clusters of peaks. The Tibetan highland is a vast and relatively barren land of snow, bare rock, and almost useless country from the normal human point of view. It does serve, however, to protect most of the Orient from cold Arctic winter storms, it does condition the climatic subsystems of the southeastern section of the continent, and it does orient the drainage of the great rivers that pour into the lowlands of the continental margins. The great highland mass also forms a curtain wall around one of the large units of the Orient, the Indian sub-continent.

The Indian subcontinent is one of the ancient land masses of the earth, a triangular unit that extends southward toward the equator for well over a thousand miles. The base of the triangle lies across the north, and between its hard rock and the high mountains of the Tibetan highland there extends a great lowland trough being filled with alluvium from the highland by several river systems. This trough, the North India Plain, is thought of chiefly as the valleys of three great river systems, the Indus on the west, the Ganges in the center, and the Brahmaputra in the east. These drain out to the west and to the east in two large estuarine deltas at either northern corner of the peninsula. The Indian Peninsula is tilted toward the east, and most of its streams drain toward the east coast, building small deltas at their mouths. The west coast from the sea appears as a low mountain range fronting on a very narrow coastal plain. The island of Ceylon is offset on the east side, near the southern tip of the peninsula. The Indian subcontinent is ocean-flanked on two sides, by the Arabian Sea on the west and Gulf of Bengal on the east. Within this curtain-framed zone lie the large states of India and Pakistan, the fought-over area of Kashmir, and the small states of Nepal, Bhutan, and Ceylon. Off the southern peninsular west coast lies the miniscule area of the Maldive Islands, an elongated chain of coral atolls.

To the southeast, from our high Tibetan perch, the curving ranges of the great mountain system bend southward sharply on the Tibetan corner of India-China, and through them in narrow canyons flow several of the great rivers of the peninsular corner of the continent, the Irrawaddy, Salween, Chao Phraya, Mekong, and Song Hoi. After the southward bend the mountain ranges flare apart as they extend southward, their altitudes decrease, and the river valleys grow broader, ending in delta fills in estuaries and bays. This alternating pattern of ranges and river valleys separates the peninsular corner into a series of range-framed lowlands, each containing a minor plateau or platform set against a mountain chain. One of the principal ranges extends far to the south, forming the backbone of the Malay Peninsula. The lower, delta sectors of these several lowlands long formed very wet and marshy tracts, heavily flooded during the late rainy season, but they have all had drainage canal systems built into them

PRIMARY ELEMENTS OF FOLDING,
FAULTING, AND MOUNTAIN BUILDING.

STRUCTURAL LOWLANDS AND BASINS.

POSITION OF THE OBSERVER
PER TEXTUAL COMMENTARY.

IRAN

AFGHANISTAN

PAKISTAN

INDIA

Arabian
Sea

Bay
of
Bengal

INDIAN   OCEAN

CEYLON

*the geomorphic skeleton
of the oriental world*

2

| 0 | | 500 | | 1000 miles |
| 0 | | | | 1000 kilometers |

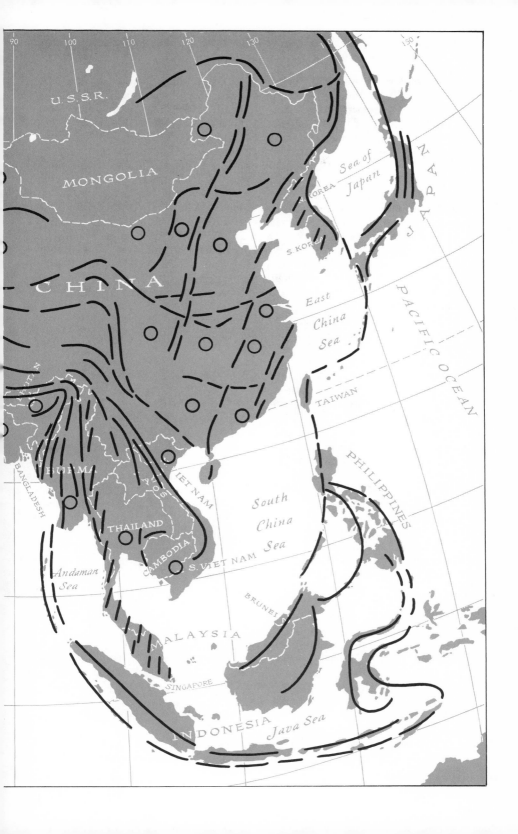

in the modern period. Within this series of mountain-framed units lie the modern political states of Burma, Thailand, Laos, Cambodia, North Vietnam, South Vietnam, West Malaysia, and the island state of Singapore at the southern tip of the Malay Peninsula.

To the east, from the Tibetan viewpoint, there lies a real jumble of ranges and basins, hilly country, and riverine lowlands forming mainland China. The northern Tibetan ranges chiefly follow the southward bend of the southern ranges, and these extend southeastward across westernmost China proper. Beyond them, to the east, lie a series of northeast-southwest mountain range systems, spaced at intervals toward the China coast. There are four members in this series, each set somewhat lower in altitude as one looks eastward to the China Sea. The range systems are not fully continuous in extent, have many separate members, and display different patterns of relief. Cutting across them in crudely east-west directions are four other widely spaced range systems extending from the western highlands to the coastal bays and seas of the western Pacific Ocean. The northernmost range system in this series lies in the far north against the borders of Soviet Siberia, and the southernmost is but a short system that appears only as the drainage divide between two river systems in southern China.

The cumulative effect of this double system of mountain ranges is to divide China proper into a series of alternating units of highland and lowland, for the spaces between the range systems are chiefly structural basins of subsidence, lowlands set at different altitudes that, for the most part, now are being filled with alluvium by the great river systems that drain from the heart of Asia into the western Pacific. The northern sector is more widely spaced, with larger units of lowland between the ranges, whereas much of China south of the Yangtze River seems to appear chiefly as jumbled hill country, with but small patches of lowlands irregularly set among the masses of hills. The Amur River system drains the far north into northern Pacific waters, the great Huang Ho follows an irregular course across northern China, the Yangtze River system, largest in drainage basin and carrying the most water, drains the central eastern section of Tibet and the main basins of central China, and the southern West River system drains a smaller and narrower section of south China. Numerous smaller streams drain the eastern coastal lands of China in smaller blocks, set between the master streams.

Offset, across a subsiding basin now occupied by the Yellow Sea, lies the 600 mile-long peninsula of Korea. In earlier geologic time mountain building on the eastern Asian mainland warped and folded Korea into the systems of mainland China, but the later subsidence of northern basin units created a peninsula attached to the mainland only at the high northern end. The Korean Peninsula is tilted to the west, with a mountain range system fronting the Japan Sea on the east, the coastal reach aligned in accord with one of the Pacific island arcs. The west and south coasts slope into the Yellow Sea, and this section is fringed by hundreds of islands, islets, mud flats, and bare rocks.

Beyond the irregular mainland fringes of this corner of Asia there extend several series of large and small islands, set on great curving arcs.

The westernmost of these island arcs commences south of Burma, in line with the terminal curving ranges between Burma and India. The structural lines extend from the Andaman Islands through Sumatra where the arc lines bend eastward and continue into eastern Indonesia. In eastern Indonesia two sets of master arcs approach each other but do not cross. The Andaman-to-Celebes arc lines swing northward around Borneo in a double curve that extends through the Philippines to a buttress in Taiwan. From Taiwan another pair of arcs curves northward into Japan, where still other arcs branch northward into the northern Japanese island of Hokkaido, with a final arc structure ranging still farther northward toward the Kamchatkan Peninsula. An eastern set of arc lines extends from eastern New Guinea westward through the long length of that island, breaking sharply northward in locally contorted curves through the island cluster of Halmahera, in eastern Indonesia, from which point the arc lines swing out into the Pacific Ocean, extend northward through the Mariana Islands, and curve back into central Japan.

Both sets of these double island arcs are the master structural lines along which folding, faulting, vulcanism, and volcanism have built islands repeatedly, submerged them, and rebuilt them, enclosing units of sedimentary rocks lifted above sea level. One line within each master pair is geologically the more active, for hundreds of volcanoes cap many of the islands with their graceful curving lines. Most of the hundreds of volcanoes now are inactive, but scattered along the arcs are dozens of live and active volcanoes. In the present construct, at present sea level, nearly 20,000 islands, islets, rocks, and little coral reefs make up this island world. The dozen quite large islands, such as Sumatra, Luzon, or Honshu, all are rather complex physical structures, having ancient intrusives, old sedimentary rocks, young volcanics, and coastal fringes of recent alluvial sedimentation; each is cut through by several primary fault zones into major blocks, and each is riven by numerous minor fault zones; each is a variable complex of high mountains, internal structure valleys, peninsular appendages, and coastal plains. Many of the smaller islands are marginal offshore members of main-island uplands, now set apart by the present stand of sea level. Some islands are but volcanoes built above present sea level. Some southern islands have solid bases just below present sea level and appear as lacelike and ephemeral coral atolls barely above present sea level. Bays, gulfs, and small seas occupy spaces between island groups, and there are large expanses of rather shallow water between the Asian mainland and the island chains. The two deepest oceanic trenches, the Mindanao Deep and the Japan Trench, lie just off eastern Mindanao and Honshu, respectively. Essentially, all the islands, as we see them today with sea level at its present stand, are but the tops of larger rock masses reaching upward from the Pacific Ocean floor. The numbers of islands, their shapes, and the lowland extents have varied greatly in Pleistocene and Recent geological time, according to the height of sea level.

The island world is not only a zone in which scattered volcanoes currently become active, but it is also a shaky world in which earthquake tremors are very frequent in most sectors, and in which occasional hard shakes cause widespread destruction to the present land portions occupied by human settlement. Within this island world are the large political states of Indonesia, the Philippines, Japan, and the eastermost political unit Papua-Northeast New Guinea (discussed in Thomas L. McKnight, *Australia's Corner of the World,* another book in this series). There are also small political units occupying niches in the island arcs: Portuguese Timor, the protected state of Brunei, and the island bastion of Taiwan.

The Warm and Wet Monsoon World

Climatically, most of the Orient falls into the region that is often termed the "monsoon world." Here, for most of the year one is impressed that the daily weather is warm to hot, muggy to that dripping-wet feeling, and one keeps an electric bulb turned on in the wardrobe to fend off the mildews and molds. The period before the seasonal rains set in is, in sensible terms, the worst part of the year, when temperatures, humidities, and human tempers build up to heights of acute human discomfort. Then "the rains" bring slightly lower temperatures but not lower humidities, and life endures, perspiringly. Gradually lowering humidities and temperatures follow toward the ends of the rainy seasons, and there is even an occasional early morning during the "winter" when it becomes almost cool and quite enjoyable to the European, though the local native populace may declare that it is "freezing cold." The three-season weather cycle (hot-dry, warm-wet, and cooler-dry) is operative for most portions of the lowland Orient, with varying timings on the onset of the rains and the cool season. The annual weather cycle has selective elements of drama in different regions. The west coast of India awaits the onset of the summer monsoon rains with nervous expectancy regarding its earliness or lateness and its seasonal adequacy, a short period of daily false thundershowers often preceding that day when the clouds burst and the land becomes wet and then turns green with fresh plant growth. The approach of autumn in the Philippines often brings about an equivalent nervous expectancy as to whether the typhoon approaching out of the Pacific Ocean will create a big disaster or only a little one. Hong Kong and southern China nervously await the news of the path of the typhoon: Will it swing sharply northward over Taiwan and into Japan, will it head for the China coast, or will it turn southward toward the Gulf of Tonking and northern Vietnam?

In more conventional terms, the monsoon world is one in which the annual weather cycle is dominated by two primary seasonal air-drift patterns, a summer drift from the oceanic regions toward the mainland interior, followed by a relatively quiet period, and a winter drift off the mainland into the oceanic regions, followed by another quiet period, though this is an oversimplification (Fig. 3). The summer monsoon is one in which warm and moist air out of the Indian and Pacific oceans moves primarily northward over the island arcs and onto the mainlands of Asia, with different air-mass components operative in separate directional movements around the several mainland fringes. The summer monsoon commences anywhere from late May to mid-July, depending on the locality. Sometimes commencing with a burst in one area, its onset is inconspicuous in another, and the seasonal drift tapers off in September-October, so that a quiet period of cooling and drying out sets in. The winter monsoon is one in which dry and cool-to-cold air moves chiefly southward out of the interiors of the fringes of the mainland toward and sometimes across the nearer of the island arcs. Thundershowers tend to be frequent during the summers in the inland and northern sectors, but they may occur the year round in the southernmost of the island arcs. Winter rains tend to be frontal rains in China, Korea, and Japan. The monsoon system is really a very complex hemispheric system of heat and moisture adjustment between the northern and southern hemispheres of the earth, and its local surface happenings (wind, cloud, and rain) are details in this wholesale adjustment system, for most of the causal factors and major elements of seasonal shift relate to the upper atmosphere.

Throughout the whole of the Orient there are highland units that project above the surface lowlands, and above about 5,000 feet altitude most of the unpleasantness of the Orient's climate is gone since the tropical highlands have rather pleasant weather almost throughout the year. As the higher ranges of northern Burma project to still greater altitudes winters properly appear, with snow and freezing conditions, and there is a strong contrast between summer and winter. The Tibetan and Mongolian highlands, of course, also have this strong seasonal contrast but here the summer is shorter and is the less spectacular of the two seasonal intervals. From the Yangtze Valley northward, on the mainland, for all of Korea, and from central Japan northward, winter conditions are not at all mild and not at all like those of the rest of the Orient. In these northern sectors the period from October through April is likely to be punctuated by alternations of winter cyclonic weather in the pattern familiar to northern United States, with cold, stormy intervals giving way to short periods of sunny but cold days. North China lowland areas receive little precipitation at this time, but Korea and northern Japan may receive heavy snowfalls, and the winter scene in Hokkaido is likely to resemble that of New England. Western China and Szechwan and Kueichou provinces suffer the ponding of moist air in the lee of the Tibetan highland, have rather high ratios of winter cloudiness, and receive the lowest insolation values of any portion of the Orient.

Although the separate components of the summer monsoon operate differently, in terms of mechanics, timing, and meteorologic causation, there are general conditions that often are similar in effect. The seasonal timing of the onset of the rains is irregular, the annual volume of moisture supplied to the land areas varies greatly, the depth of penetration into the Eurasian mainland is annually quite variable, precise weather sequences differ from year to year, and the annual number and ferocity of typhoons in the western Pacific and tropical cyclones in the Bay of Bengal (both being hurricanes in American English) are somewhat variable. (The two most destructive storms in modern weather history struck the central Philippines and Bangladesh (to use the current place name), in November, 1970.) All this variability means that in any one year there may be drought, severe flooding, or both, in almost all areas. The southeastern peninsular corner of Eurasia rarely suffers severe drought, but it

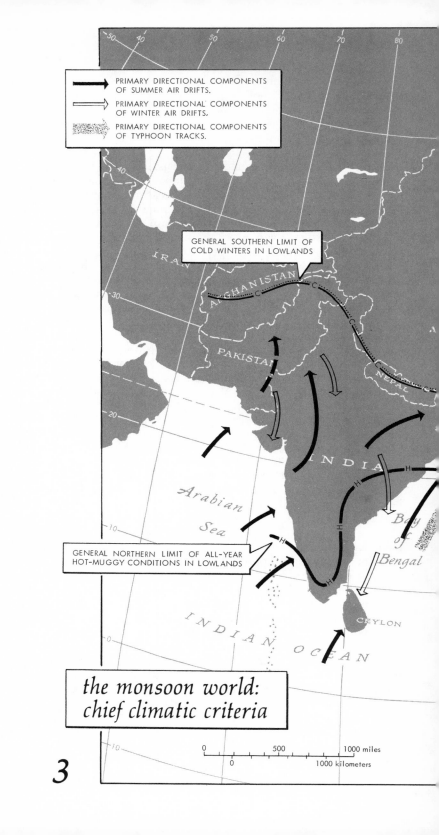

PRIMARY DIRECTIONAL COMPONENTS
OF SUMMER AIR DRIFTS.

PRIMARY DIRECTIONAL COMPONENTS
OF WINTER AIR DRIFTS.

PRIMARY DIRECTIONAL COMPONENTS
OF TYPHOON TRACKS.

GENERAL SOUTHERN LIMIT OF
COLD WINTERS IN LOWLANDS

GENERAL NORTHERN LIMIT OF ALL-YEAR
HOT-MUGGY CONDITIONS IN LOWLANDS

IRAN

AFGHANISTAN

PAKISTAN

NEPAL

INDIA

Arabian
Sea

Bay
of
Bengal

INDIAN OCEAN

CEYLON

*the monsoon world:
chief climatic criteria*

0   500   1000 miles

0   1000 kilometers

3

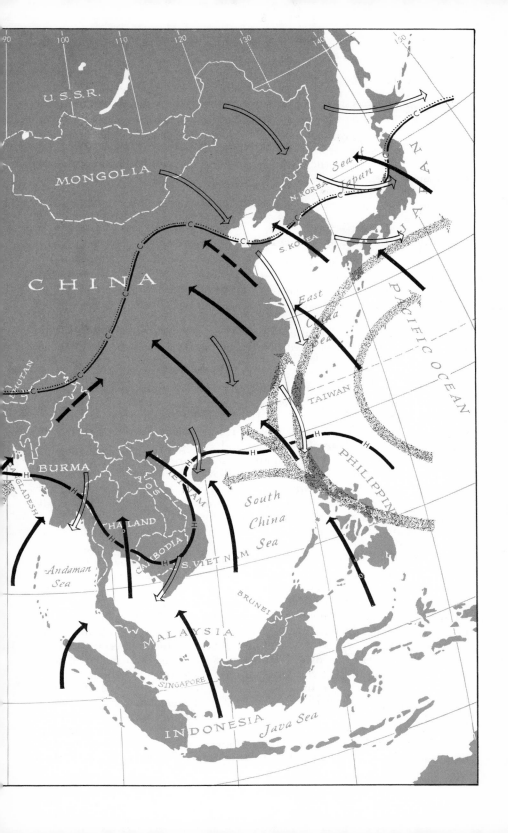

may suffer from excessive precipitation, causing abnormal flooding. Central to northwestern India-Pakistan and central and north China are both drier margins on which the annual hazard from summer monsoon irregularity is so great that for agriculture the annual hazard is always present and occasionally almost disastrous. It is commonly thought that the island sectors seldom suffer from such variability, but this is untrue. Climatic regionalism throughout the island world is complex and localized because of the acute variation in local exposure to the seasonal wind systems, but there are many small regions in which the annual hazard, from drought to excessive precipitation, affect human living systems.

Plants, Animals, and Land and Water Control

The biotic world lives within the framework of the physical world and, since the physical environment of the Orient is one of the richer and more varied of those on the surface of our earth, so the biotic worlds of plants and animals are two of the richer complexes. Man, transcending the animal world, has not been content with the nature-produced physical and biotic worlds, but has altered both these in major terms. This section will deal only very briefly with the plant and animal worlds and with what man has done to alter the elemental patterns of the physical environment.

In terms of wild plants of all kinds, the Orient has a wide reach, from the Sino-Japanese province of the northern, cool-to-cold Palearctic realm in northern Manchuria and Hokkaido, to the Malaysian province of the hot and humid Oriental realm in Malaysia and Indonesia, and to the dry but cold-wintered Tibetan and Mongolian provinces of the Palearctic realm (Fig. 4). In more common terms this means a range from the almost pure stands of the coniferous forests of the north containing few plants of direct dietary value to man, through the exotic and multiple-specied splendor of the tropical rain forests rich in plants that man could use for food and other needs, to the very spare-specied and stunted scantness of the Tibetan highland and the desert basins of central Asia. There are regions wherein several plant complexes merge in the locally variable environmental niches, as in the Loess Highlands of North China, with its northern forests on the mountains, its grassy-shrubby elements on the dry, open loesslands, and its hardy subtropicals in protected spots. The corner of the Tibetan highlands where India, Burma, and China join is another such meeting ground, ranging from the tropical niches of the deep river canyons through the tropical highland mid-altitudes to the margins of the alpine zones on the higher mountains. Perhaps the Orient has over 100,000 species of the higher plants, plus many more thousands of the lower plants. Although early human occupants of the Orient were unconcerned with forests as sources of timber and wood pulp, they were vitally involved in canvassing the ranges of plants yielding edible roots, leaves, berries, fruits, and nuts and those plants yielding string and cordage, dyes, fish intoxicants, medicinals, and plants useful in making magic. Modern man takes pleasure in the thousands of orchids and the hundreds of other decorative plants he has taken into his gardens and hothouses, but he also utilizes the products of a wide range of commercially useful plants in his manufacturing processes.

At some early point domestication of wild plants began in several regional sectors of the Orient, and we now recognize within the broad region several zones of domestication-evolution of cropping systems. South China-Vietnam, Malaysia-Sumatra-Java, Eastern India, and North China are such zones in which numbers of grasses, legumes, herbs, and trees yielded crop plants of significant value. The Philippines and eastern Indonesia-New Guinea are minor centers. Northwestern India-Pakistan shares with the whole of the Middle East in being one of the productive centers of crop plants and plant-growing systems. Large numbers of the crop and decorative plants have been taken widely over the rest of the world, as the gardener recognizes the regional origins of such varied decorative plants as the chrysanthemums, azaleas, cammelias, and the orchids, as the farmer recognizes those same regional origins in the millets, rices, bananas, citruses, walnuts, and mangoes, and as the dietary epicure recognizes the regional origins of the spicy vine peppers, nutmeg, cardamon, safflower, and turmeric. Although many New World plants have been added to the crop lists of regions of the Orient, much of the productive agriculture of the Orient still hinges around plants native to the home realms.

People have been living in the Orient for a long expanse of time, and but little of the wild plant growth remains in its natural distributional and spatial systems because man has been turning the countrysides into cultivated farmscapes and village and town settlements. Patches of relatively undisturbed forest do remain in a few corners, and there still are large areas of wild forest, but no longer are they virgin, for they have been cut over by shifting cultivators time and again and combed for their special products by repeated generations of forest exploiters. A few species are now extinct, numerous others remain only within the confines of temple gardens, and many more species are reduced to lesser numbers in hunted-through territories. However, in this generally warm and humid environment, plants regain their own whenever man slackens his efforts, plant growth is rapid and profuse, and many once occupied sites repeatedly have become so overgrown that the earlier human imprints are fully disguised. In many areas man has long tolerated certain forms of wild growth, and there remained sufficient seed stock that nature could often maintain a semblance of its own until human effort slackened and the spread of the wild cover was once again allowed. Many portions of the Orient, particularly India and China, today are extremely short of the large forests that now are so valuable to civilised and complex industrial-use systems.

Within the animal world the Orient belongs chiefly to the Oriental Region, reaching from west of the Indus River eastward along the upper altitudes of the Himalaya Mountains to the China Sea slightly south of the Yangtze River mouth, and eastward in the Indies into Wallacea. The latter is a transition zone between the Oriental Region and the Australian Region, with Wallacea falling between Java and New Guinea. The northern sector of the Orient, that is North China, Korea, and Japan, falls into

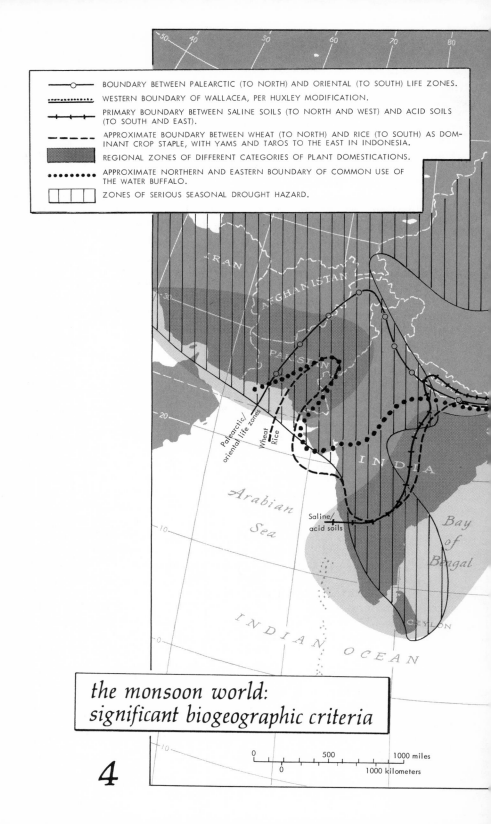

BOUNDARY BETWEEN PALEARCTIC (TO NORTH) AND ORIENTAL (TO SOUTH) LIFE ZONES.

WESTERN BOUNDARY OF WALLACEA, PER HUXLEY MODIFICATION.

PRIMARY BOUNDARY BETWEEN SALINE SOILS (TO NORTH AND WEST) AND ACID SOILS (TO SOUTH AND EAST).

APPROXIMATE BOUNDARY BETWEEN WHEAT (TO NORTH) AND RICE (TO SOUTH) AS DOMINANT CROP STAPLE, WITH YAMS AND TAROS TO THE EAST IN INDONESIA.

REGIONAL ZONES OF DIFFERENT CATEGORIES OF PLANT DOMESTICATIONS.

APPROXIMATE NORTHERN AND EASTERN BOUNDARY OF COMMON USE OF THE WATER BUFFALO.

ZONES OF SERIOUS SEASONAL DROUGHT HAZARD.

the monsoon world:
significant biogeographic criteria

4

0   500   1000 miles

0   1000 kilometers

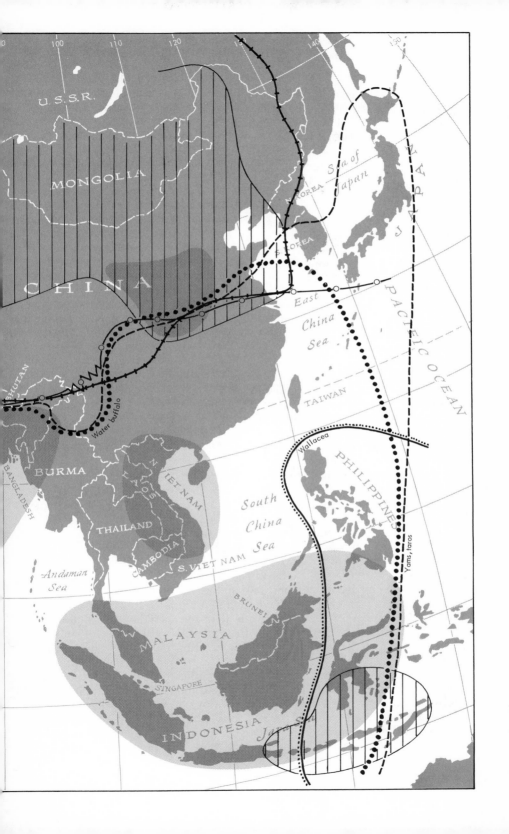

the Palearctic Region, correlating with the Palearctic realm in the plant world. Within the Orient, by the inclusion of avian and marine life forms, there is a rich assemblage of wild animal life. From these regions have come many of the pet and zoo animals now widely known around the earth, although some are so scarce today in their homelands that they require zoo breeding for their maintenance. Much of the Orient formerly was big game hunting territory, but the modern inroads on the animal population have reduced these prospects. Many of the species are small in size, of interest to the zoologist but seldom seen by the local populace or the visitor. Territorial ranges have often been restricted by the expansion of the cultivated farmscapes or the hunting efficiencies of the simpler cultures occupying the rough country. The evolved taboo on animal killing among the religious communities of Hindus and Buddhists, however, has perpetuated populations of many animal forms in southern and southeastern Asia.

Out of the wealth of animal forms within the Orient a significant series of domestications took place that added to the earthly population of birds, pets, and livestock. The Zebu strains of cattle, the water buffalo, and the elephant are the notable large animals, but many of the ducks, geese, and pheasants, and the whole of the group of chickens and pea-fowls, as well as a large series of pet birds and the goldfishes, come out of the Orient. The Siamese and Burmese cat population of the world at large derives from the two namesake countries. Although technically still wild in the proper sense, the many fish species raised in ponds throughout the Orient are selective choices of wild life utilized for human living systems.

As the agricultural systems of the Orient matured there evolved in different regions varied systems of modifying potential landscapes to patterns of greater utility to man. The most notable of these efforts resulted in the system of wet-field terracing, focussed around the growing of rice as a primary crop plant, to be seen in every country in the Orient today. Several different kinds of field terracing are found almost everywhere in the Orient today, from the spectacular (but not really significant) terraces of northern Luzon in the Philippines, to the crude dryfield terracing of almost any hill region in the Orient, and to the crude restorative land-reclamation erosion-control ditch-terraces constructed in historically evolved badland portions of the Loess Highlands of northwestern China. Terracing may have modified almost a fourth of the total agricultural acreage of the Orient. The field terraces themselves are but one part of the wet-field systems, for the integrated water control systems that feed most of the wet-field terraces are often impressive engineering operations.

The diking and drainage systems of China probably are the next most impressive features of modification. Commencing as simple flood control dikes along a few streams in the culture hearth of northern China, dike systems now line most of the rivers of lowland China; that they have been carefully maintained, expanded in protective coverage, and are again being expanded in contemporary time has provided continuing modification of the lowlands of China. Indian diking is probably at least as old, but the continuity of maintenance of dike systems in India has been far less, and modern flood control problems provoke greater trouble. In the great deltas of Southeast Asia it was only in the nineteenth century that diking and drainage canal systems were installed, but these works opened the deltas to permanent settlement in permanent modification of the riverine landscapes.

Irrigation systems are very old in the Orient. Reservoirs predate history in India, where the creation of small artificial lakes behind dam embankments (termed tanks in Indian English) permitted both down-grade subsoil water seepage to support village orchards located just below the reservoirs and irrigation canals distributing water to more distant crop fields. Thousands of reservoirs have held water in the local land-scapes of India, Pakistan, and Ceylon during the dry seasons, making them permanently inhabitable by agricultural populations dispersed throughout the landscapes. Irrigation systems in North China did not utilize the reservoir, but canal diversion systems tapping seasonal rivers date very far back. Elsewhere, most irrigation systems are much more modern and may be culminated by the Lower Mekong River Basin multipurpose water control systems of Thailand, Cambodia, Laos, and South Vietnam.

A singular item in land control, in the broad sense, is the Chinese development of fertilizer-soil maintenance systems, the most advanced of any portion of the Orient in early times. The use of crop rotation, animal manures, green manuring by plowing under young plant growth, the rotational growing of nitrogen-fixing legumes, the crumbling and leaching of old pounded-earth and sun-dried brick walls for their nitrates, and the use of composted materials on fields all date back at least to the early centuries of the Christian Era. There is no documentary proof of the very early use of nightsoil and other sewage, but it is clear that such materials have regularly been part of the fertilizer routine for at least a thousand years. Many other equivalent techniques have been added since then, and Chinese farming practices, when permitted by the pressures on the land, have long been among the best in the world at maintaining the productive quality of farm land; these Chinese practices have also often turned poor soils into productive soils, and many old Chinese settlements are surrounded by zones of richer-than-natural belts of very productive soils.

Elsewhere in the Orient farmers have, historically, and for the most part, been less careful husbandmen in handling the soils that provide their living. Oriental agricultural systems often have matured out of shifting cultivation in which specific care for the soil was not a tech-nologic procedure. Both in earlier periods and in the modern period soil erosion has taken its toll, and no part of the Orient has escaped the historic process of destructive erosion of land surfaces smooth enough to provide sites for agriculture. In recent centuries from Korea around to Pakistan the pressures of men upon the land have pushed cropping right to the tops of much of the hill country. In areas in which irrigation is old there sometimes has occurred the waterlogging of soils, as in parts of western India and Pakistan, to the end that many croppable localities have become over saline and now are nonproductive.

Peoples and Systems of Culture

The Orient possesses an immense variety of peoples who derive from separate specific origins and who speak close to 1,000 languages. The world's leading language by number of speakers is Mandarin Chinese, used from northern Manchuria into southwestern China by well over 600 million people. Six other languages [Japanese, Hindi, Indonesian Malay, Bengali, Shanghai (Wu), and Urdu] are spoken by over 50 million people each, in descending order of importance. Still another ten languages are spoken by over 20 million people each, Korean, Cantonese, Vietnamese, Thai, Burmese, Telegu, Tamil, Marathi, Gujarati, and Punjabi. Of these, three are Chinese languages (Mandarin, Shanghai, and Cantonese), eight are Indian languages (Hindi, Bengali, Urdu, Telegu, Tamil, Marathi, Gujarati, and Punjabi), and the other six represent single national cultures (Japanese, Korean, Malay, Vietnamese, Thai, and Burmese). These seventeen languages account for the great majority of the population of the Orient, but there are another group of at least twenty separate languages spoken by anywhere from one to fifteen million people each, with the groups distributed from Mongolia to Ceylon. At the lower end of the frequency scale, of course, are at least one hundred languages spoken by less than one hundred people each; these languages are in the process of disappearing.

Language, of course, is not an accurate indication of ethnic origins or relationships, for many small ethnic groups in the Orient have lost and no longer speak their own native tongues, but speak languages of their neighbors. If one admits the use of the older, standard ethnic classification, the peoples of the Orient derive from all three major racial gene pools, Congoid, Caucasoid, and Mongoloid, with the Mongoloid peoples by far outnumbering those of other origins. Congoid peoples long ago were scattered thinly across the southern margins of the Orient, their black skin pigmentation remaining as a residual element among many groups of the southernmost sectors, but today Congoid ethnic groups are but small and remnantal. In the Orient Caucasoid peoples are chiefly represented in India-Pakistan, having deeply penetrated the Indian subcontinent, but they enter the ethnic complexity of Chinese Central Asia, are represented in such far-reaching migratory movements as the Ainu remnant of northern Japan, and then are present in the modern intermarriage mixes produced by modern European scattering in all parts of the Orient.

The Chinese, historically, have paid little attention to strict matters of racial discrimination, for anyone who adopts Chinese ways in the end becomes Chinese, and Chinese only distinguish nonChinese in terms of culture systems. Although the same can be said in parts of India, there always has been social consciousness of ethnic origins and relations in the Indian world view. A modern Burmese-speaking citizen of Burma may actually derive from any of several different specific ethnic stocks, as may a Tagalog-speaking Filipino.

National culture systems have tended to gloss over the differences between ethnic and cultural groups derived from different gene pools and culture hearths (Fig. 5). It is very evident in the Orient, however, that the glossing over, melting pot, ethnic mixing processes have nowhere become complete for, despite the modern attempts to establish national systems of culture corresponding to the outlines of national political states, every country in the Orient possesses larger or smaller numbers of culture groups adhering to some subsystem that involves language, manner of dress, social complexes, and ways of thinking. Japan and Korea are the nearest approaches to linguistic and ethnic homogeneity within each national culture system. The Korean case is in jeopardy, however, for if the line of division between North and South Korea continues much longer, there will be two culture systems and there may also begin the separation of language systems, for communist and noncommunist portions of the country now are following divergent ideologies requiring semantic clarification, each in its own terms.

Nowhere is this matter of ethnic mix and linguistic variety shown more clearly than in the shatter-belt zone of the southeastern corner of the continent and its nearby island fringes. For several thousand years different culture groups have been moving into this corner sector to compete for space in the lowlands and to occupy fractionated niches in the hill and mountain country, with near-relatives scattered in discontinuous groupings over a wide area. Beyond that kind of mixture-separation, the two dominant culture worlds of China and India have diffused their culture systems into the southeastern zone in overlapping spatial terms (see Fig. 5). The diffusion of the Chinese culture world into the shatter-belt zone contributed only one broadly generic culture system, but the Indian system diffused under different religious motivations (Hindu, Buddhist, and Islamic) to the end that there are different Indian culture subsystems exerting pressures on all other systems and subsystems in the shatter-belt zone.

The aspects of mixing of culture systems in Southeast Asia were carried further, of course, by the coming of the European who established what finally became political colonial holdings. Into these areas different European nationalities interjected different languages, cultural mores, political systems, and social organizational elements. The Filipinos first became Hispanicised Roman Catholics except for those who lived in a few pagan island interiors and a minority of Islamic "Moros" in the southernmost islands, but then they became Americanized to the end that the Philippines today is the third largest English-speaking country in the world. At the same time the French were teaching the French language and French customs to peoples in what was Indochina, the Malays were absorbing British customs and British English, and in Indonesia the prevading influence was in the direction of Dutch characteristics. This kind of differential cultural orientation has not often affected whole

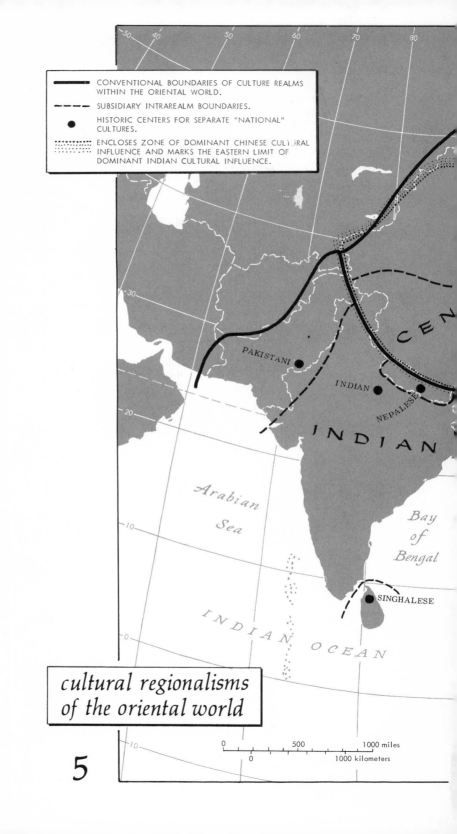

CONVENTIONAL BOUNDARIES OF CULTURE REALMS WITHIN THE ORIENTAL WORLD.

SUBSIDIARY INTRAREALM BOUNDARIES.

HISTORIC CENTERS FOR SEPARATE "NATIONAL" CULTURES.

ENCLOSES ZONE OF DOMINANT CHINESE CULTURAL INFLUENCE AND MARKS THE EASTERN LIMIT OF DOMINANT INDIAN CULTURAL INFLUENCE.

PAKISTANI

INDIAN

NEPALESE

CEN

INDIAN

Arabian

Sea

Bay of Bengal

SINGHALESE

INDIAN OCEAN

cultural regionalisms of the oriental world

| 0 | 500 | 1000 miles |
| 0 | | 1000 kilometers |

5

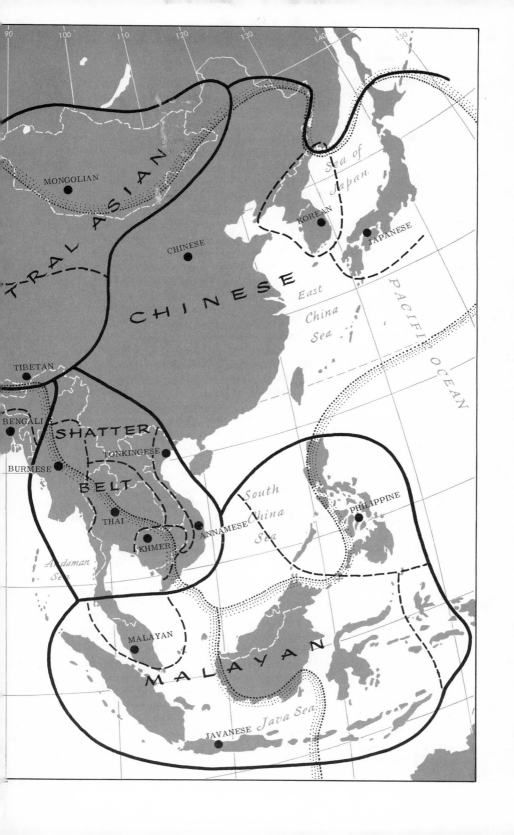

populations, but it did influence legal-political systems, second-language orientation, consumer goods preferences, and regional ties, perhaps penetrating most deeply in the Philippines. In China the influences of many occidental cultures exerted differential regional and economic class patterns, but Korea and Japan held aloof from all occidental contacts until late in the nineteenth century. It is in southern, but particularly in southeastern, Asia that this added veneer has reinforced the differential elements of culture in the traditional patterns of shatter-belt conditions.

Since the end of World War II the postcolonial trends have, of course, been toward political and cultural nationalisms everywhere in the Orient with quite varied trends, developments, and results. Japan, almost prostrate at the end of World War II, has made the strongest recovery by far, but Japan is clearly the most culturally unified country and has had fewer internal problems in determining her own future cultural identity, economic direction, and politico-social processes. Vietnam, on the other hand, is a region in which, in the past, there have been internal ethnic dissensions, mixed religious directions, divergent political trends, and several regional cohesions. Since World War II Vietnam has been torn by contradictory politico-economic trends between members of the dominant ethnic group, the Vietnamese, but there are many minority hill country groups, often simply labelled Montagnards, to whom recent military activities represent only frustrating conditions in which they become pawns in a power struggle. India is a single national political state now occupying a major portion of a regional physical environment, but there are many divergent trends within India in which regionalisms, ethnic disparities, political aspirations, social problems, and discordant economic levels make political unanimity and economic development very hard to achieve.

The pressures of the modern world are toward political nationalisms, despite the growing trends toward the "one-world concept," and political nationalism comes hard in regions inhabited by many different ethnic groups that possess dissimilar culture systems. Nowhere is this more clearly seen than in Burma today. The lowland Burmese have long been creating a Burmese culture, but the political state includes many sizable groups that are neither Burmese in ethnic origin nor Burmese in culture. Such ethnic groups as the Chin, Kachin, Karen, Palaung, and Shan are both ethnic and cultural minorities in a modern political state that does not yield in its Burmese nationalistic aspirations to create a Burmese state and culture that is chiefly Burmese in orientation.

The two primary oriental culture systems, Chinese and Indian, have exerted strong influences on all other regions of the Orient to the end that one, the other, or both have affected the culture system of the regions that now appear as independent political states. Korea and Japan bear the Chinese imprint, as Ceylon and Indonesia bear the Indian imprint, and as Thailand, Cambodia, and Vietnam bear the imprints of both. Later Islamic influences show up in the separation of Pakistan from India, in the Islamization of the Malays in Malaysia and Indonesia. In the modern period the occidental cultures have imparted varying imprints on several regional cultures. In the modern period, too, there is the impact of China upon the Philippines, Thailand, Malaysia, and Indonesia through immigrant settlement, with India contributing to Malaysia and to Ceylon. Although the Orient constitutes one very large unit in the cultural differentiation of the earth, the Oriental culture realm, that culture realm involves a large number of subregional entities that are now showing up as separate political states.

CHAPTER 2 *environments and landscapes*

In the conceptual fiction of many an occidental "The Orient" is thought to possess a landscape full of strange architecture fitted with labyrinthine alleys that terminate in hidden doorways behind which strange things happen, and it constitutes an environment compelling strange kinds of reaction systems in its peoples, making them into the "different" sorts that fit our mental "pictures" of what the Orient must be. One can search out and find localities and behavior patterns that conform to the occidental perception of the Orient, of course, but these conceptual structures are not very real in broad and general terms. The Orient is made up of the same kinds of physical landscapes as are found in the Occident, and environmental influences in the Orient operate to about the same degree that they do in other parts of the earth. That is, the Orient is composed of mountains, hills, river valleys, plains, coastal fringes, and islands of rock, sand, silt, and clay; there are humid rainy localities in which it rains throughout the year, there are seasonally wet and dry weather cycles, there are mountains that receive lots of snow and a few lowlands in which snowdrifts pile up, and there are regions in which rainfall is scarce and water is hard to find; and the sultry heat of an oriental summer night carries no more mystical influences than does such a night in southern Florida. The Orient is part of our one earth in respect to its environments and landscapes, and analogues for each distinctive element of the natural scene can be found at some other point on the surface of the earth so that nothing is totally unique in the appearance, quality, or "influence" of the oriental environmental circumstance. The spatial arrangements of environments and landscapes of the southeastern corner of Asia obviously differ from those of North America or Africa in the simple sense that no two of our physical continents are shaped, arranged, or constructed alike. The Orient suffers from typhoons as southeastern North America suffers from hurricanes, the occidental terminology for the storm phenomenon being the only significant variable. Plant species and animal species differ between Southeast Asia and the corresponding sections of other continents, of course, and possibly Oriental Asia possessed the richest of all wild plant and animal complexes as man began to utilize and alter those patterns, but these plants and animals do not impart oriental influences to human beings. It is in its ethnic and cultural systems that the Orient differs from the Occident.

Varieties of Environments

In examining aspects of the separate regions of the earth, one of the more interesting problems is that of attempting to discern the nature of the separate regional environments that permitted the maturing of regional culture systems. Clearly one recognizes that there are many subsystems of culture in the Orient. What, then, is the relation between regional environments and those subsystems? Are the regional environments different enough that it is the nature of the environment, in itself, that has promoted these cultural distinctions, or are the environments simply differently shaped and sized boxes into which culture groups penetrated, there to develop their different subsystems on their own volition or initiative? The former view is that of the environmental determinist; the latter view sees in the environment no active conditioning factors that create regionalisms in human practice. This volume is written on the geographic predilection that regional environments do not in themselves impart variations in culture to occupying populations, but that there are inherent differences in culture groups that become long-term influences in their regional development of culture systems.

It is clear, however, that very early culture groups were small in size and restricted in technologies and that for generations they lived lives that were somewhat similar in context when the regional environments were at all similar. But in a large continental zone wherein separate culture groups could find homelands at all separated by physical barriers, these regional separatisms could permit full play of such innate differences as existed between culture groups, to the end that regional environments came to correspond somewhat with cultural systems. With the passage of time, the growth in population within culture groups, and the development of regional environments, the various subsystems of the Orient have matured.

What kind of regional environment provided the optimal, or effective, conditions throughout the Orient for the separate evolutionary growth of culture systems and subsystems? Can we figuratively identify such a physical region, in terms of its elemental makeup, as existing in the Orient? The following pages schematically examine the issue without any attempt at the operational precision of the mathematical model.

Since it is not in the *kinds* of environments that distinguish the Orient, it must be in the spatial arrangements, juxtapositions, distributions, and extents of environments that make the Orient distinctive among the great land regions of the earth. And it is here that particular characteristics can be examined. Although the high interior mountains and plateaus of Inner Asia are often included in the Orient as statistical tabulations of political territories, the Orient is essentially a fringe zone of the Eurasian continent. Only periodically have the peoples of that oriental fringe interjected their cultural influences and political authorities deeply into the heartland of Eurasia, despite the long-term claim to political overlordship of Tibet and Central Asia by China. Most of the oriental mainland units terminate on the inland side in high, rugged, and rough mountain zones that are quite marginal to the living systems of the great majority of the oriental population. Most of the thickly inhabited areas, and the regions of utility, are lowland areas that lie in one of three positions: (1) marginally below the Inner Asian highlands, (2) as peninsulas projecting outward into the Indian and Pacific oceans away from the continental mass, or (3) standing as island festoons beyond the peninsular projections and separated from those peninsulas by shallow seas.

As a fringe of Eurasia, then, the Orient is essentially a collection of lowlands situated in one of two positions. The larger area is that of the mainland fringe, divided into irregularly shaped blocks by mountain ranges that jut seaward from the high interior. The lesser land area, actually distributed over a larger part of the earth's surface, is the series of island archipelagoes lying to the south and east of the Eurasian continent proper. Conventionally grouped into the five major units of the East Indies, Philippines, Ryukyus, Japan, and the Kuriles, there are nearly 20,000 islands included.

We may begin with an overly simple model for a mainland regional environment and then adjust it for the cases in which it does not fit in its simplest version (Fig. 6). A bounding series of mountain ranges is set close together on the edge of the highland core, both limbs of which flare widely in projections toward the sea. Out of the core a great river flows through a mountain canyon; once into the flat lowlands between the bounding ranges it becomes a wider river navigable by many types of small craft. Old, high, gravel terraces lie astride the river near the highland core, marking the earlier era of deposition of outwash gravels at the end of the glacial era. Below these high terrace lands lie plains of recent and contemporary flooding and alluvial deposition, the modern flood plains of the open lowland. The river plain merges into an extensive wet deltaic fringe still undergoing seaward extension. The river basin today is subject to seasonal flooding, and the modern economy of the occupant population is built around these seasonal flood discharges. A plateau-like upland is wedged against one of the bounding ranges, creating a subregional pattern of variety. There are few good passes across the bounding ranges in the upper-valley sectors near the highland core, but the ranges become less lofty and less continuous in the downvalley sector, and the ranges end in sea-margin promontories. Such a regionally demarcated environment sets up a territorial space open to occupance by any immigrant population, providing variety in local conditions, ample space for expansion, and a seasonal renewal of fertility through annual flooding. From mountain height to deltaic margin the environment provides a wide range of conditions, resources, and living niches. Such a

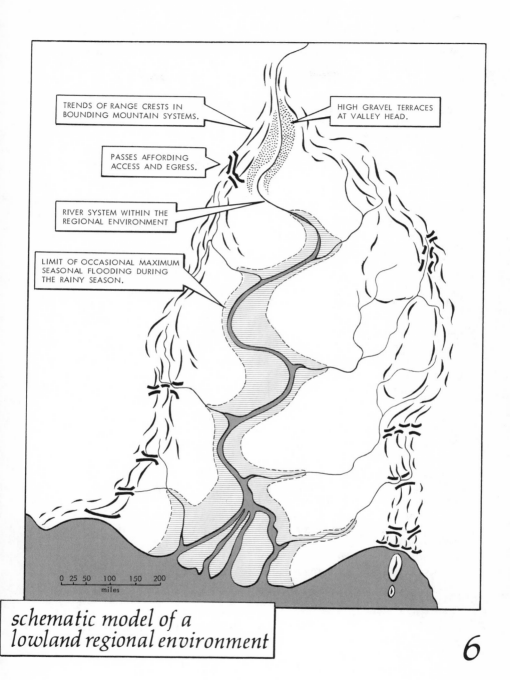

TRENDS OF RANGE CRESTS IN
BOUNDING MOUNTAIN SYSTEMS.

HIGH GRAVEL TERRACES
AT VALLEY HEAD.

PASSES AFFORDING
ACCESS AND EGRESS.

RIVER SYSTEM WITHIN THE
REGIONAL ENVIRONMENT

LIMIT OF OCCASIONAL MAXIMUM
SEASONAL FLOODING DURING
THE RAINY SEASON.

0 25 50   100   150 200
miles

*schematic model of a
lowland regional environment*

6

river basin territory was open to occupance by one or more early culture groups whether they practiced hunting-collecting, employed chiefly a fishing economy, were rudimentary crop growers, or used some combination economy. As time has passed and technologies have grown such a region gave scope for economic development, and such a region today is amenable to various patterns of utilization.

In figurative terms, such a model fits reasonably well for Burma, Thailand, or North Vietnam (Fig. 7). It does not fit so well for South Vietnam, since the second limb of the bounding frame is missing in the far south, the Mekong Delta is not thereby clearly set off, and a narrow coastal lowland is prominent in this case. Cambodia is foreshortened and does not reach full into the mountain core, and the great river does not pass through the center of the lowland flood plain, but there is a bounding frame that encloses the Tonle Sap, and the delta of the Mekong is on the seaward side. However, there are five regional environments in this mainland sector of Southeast Asia that render some variation of the figurative model and that have received historic occupance by different peoples. These five regions became the territorial bases for five modern political states, Burma, Thailand, Cambodia, North Vietnam, and South Vietnam. Each possesses some territorial integrity, each has a historic claim as a regional culture hearth, and each aspires to the status of a regional, politically controlled national culture. What modern political geographers indicate as the state of Laos is a modern anomaly since there is no satisfactory lowland territorial base in terms of the model. The lack of the model-styled base is at the core of the Laos problem, both historically and at present.

The northern sector of the India-Pakistan region comprises territorial space exemplified by the model but suitable for two regional units, for the recent filling of the great alluvial plain has buried the separating upland (the Delhi Gap) to the end that northern India-Pakistan forms one great lowland territory with three river systems and two deltaic lowlands. In environmental terms this great unit provides ample space for a very large population that could be one regional culture. It is a matter of cultural divergence that three modern political states now claim portions of the territory on the basis of a criterion that man has not been able to surmount—difference in religious systems.

India, as a large territorial unit, goes beyond the model in that the peninsula of India presents an additional physical component. The peninsula is a very old but large tilted block, sloping eastward. River systems have lightly trenched the peninsula, chiefly flowing eastward, and here one can figuratively discern a number of separate territorial spaces roughly comparable to those described by the model. However, the interstream zones are not properly mountainous, and the territorial spaces are not well separated by bounding limits. Man has found the bounds easily transgressed throughout the peninsula and, though several of the spaces have at times been units of regional occupance, peninsular India has had a very checkered history of occupance by culture groups and political groups who drew bounding lines in many ways along different features at separate times. The gross shape of the peninsula makes for an extended series of regional environments from north to south, but none of these clearly approaches the definitive unitary nature described in the model.

Korea does not fit the model at all because its chief physical bounding limit lies at the head of the peninsula and because the tilted peninsular structure enabled evolution of only short river systems draining chiefly to the west. This has created a series of small regional environments on a multiple-but-micro pattern loosely articulated along the island strewn western coast, in contrast to the single broad environment of the macro model. Nevertheless, the Koreans succeeded in forming one long-term regional unit of occupance integrated into a single culture system operating one political state.

The model breaks down in the case of China, of course, for China Proper is a very large and block-shaped spatial unit crisscrossed by two sets of structural lines that divide the total space into many units of differing physical character. All of the elements of the model are present in that there are bounding ranges, rivers, lowland flood plains, deltaic wet lowlands, and plateau-like blocks of upland. Whereas the model suggests one regional environmental unit stretching from the mountain core to the coastal sea, China Proper is so large that there are sequences of regional environments, set in series, between the highland core and the fringing seas. The North China Plain is the nearest approach to the pattern of the model, but it has independent subordinate rivers flanking the great river, both north and south of the Huang Ho. The total catchment of the Yangtze River contains several subordinate streams of major dimensions, and there are the separate regional environments of the Szechwan Basin, the Hunan Basin, the Hupei Basin, the Poyang Basin, and the Yangtze Delta. South China and Manchuria add still other units variably arranged. Instead of a single environmental region China possesses almost a dozen regional environments linked together into a compound system, with no two units fully duplicating physical conditions. Whereas the model, applied to Burma or Thailand, suggests an environment for a single culture system, the case of China suggests that this large territory might well have supplied the supporting environments for several different culture systems that could have evolved into independent political states in the modern era. This, essentially, is what happened in the European Peninsula at the other end of the Eurasian continent.

Turning to the island world off the mainland, the suggestive model becomes something different than that optimal for the mainland. Here the basic elements in the model comprise a coastal section of a largish island having a good harbor, that section backed by a coastal plain behind which there is a mountain highland from which there flows a river across the coastal plain into the harbor. Too small an island will not suffice, but a very large island may well contain several localized environments that comprise units approximating those of the model. A low island built chiefly on coral reef structure is inadequate in terms of its soils, water supply, upland core, and coastal fringe lying well above sea level. An island that is but a mountain rising out of the sea will not suffice. The climatic sequence is significant in that there must be conditions per-

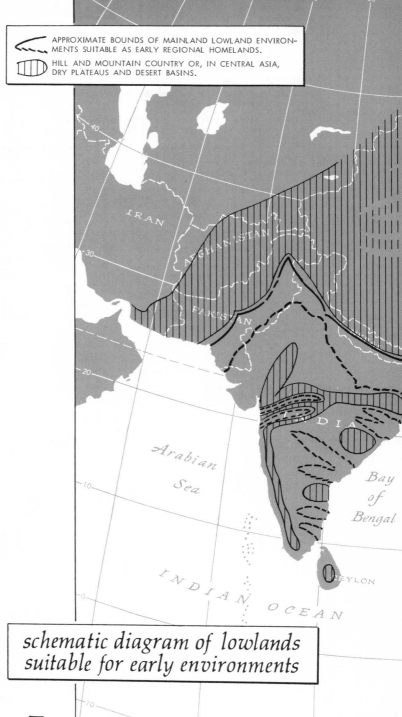

IRAN

AFGHANISTAN

PAKISTAN

INDIA

Arabian
Sea

Bay
of
Bengal

INDIAN   OCEAN

CEYLON

*schematic diagram of lowlands
suitable for early environments*

7

mitting free and easy development of plant and animal economies. In the multiple-island nature of the several archipelagoes off the Asian coast there were islands of the right conformation and climatic environment in four of the five cases, the Kurile group alone lacking the proper environmental context.

Within the 3,000 islands of the East Indies there were numerous environmental units adequate to the evolution of regional culture systems at the early stage, and the same was true in the case of the Philippines. The Ryukyu chain is of smaller proportions, but Okinawa possessed almost proper components. Among the 3,000 islands of the Japanese Archipelago there also were numerous environmental units that comprised effective regional environments. That some highlands reached far skyward in volcanic cones, that some islands contained lesser peninsulas of convoluted shape, or that dozens of islets ringed large islands were less important in the regional development of a culture system. The superfluity of islands has become significant only in modern time when extended political control came to be an issue in terms of political geography.

In the context of each archipelago the presence of several regional environments of proportions and conditions adequate to the development of a regional culture promoted rivalries, just as on the mainland, but the forms of competitive contact became those of the seaways and interisland channels rather than those of land routeways and mountain passes, so that the nature of militant history reads somewhat differently. And the offshore locations of all the archipelagoes has meant that the timing of advanced development came somewhat later than on the mainland. The long-term trends of population movements from the mainland toward the archipelagoes is part of this timing sequence, but there also is the factor of physical position on the migration routes, to the end that such islands as New Guinea and Hokkaido were far away and last in the developmental sequences. Sumatra, Java, Borneo, Mindanao, Luzon, Okinawa, Kyushu, and Honshu are the largish islands affording the effective local regional environments that came first into the patterns of human occupance by advancing culture groups.

The Malay Peninsula, of course, is the very reverse of the physical region suggested by the model. The long reach of land is narrow, irregular in surface form, and possesses no natural core-zone within which a culture group could evolve a significant cultural regionalism. Throughout most of human history the Malay Peninsula has been either a landfall point en route elsewhere or a land routeway leading away from mainland pressures. It is only in the modern era that there developed the concern for the land for itself that created the modern state of Malaysia.

Because the culture hearths and presently heavily populated regional environments are all lowland regions, they generally are similar in physical conditions. They vary, however, climatically in considerable detail within a broad range, and there are quite different plant and animal complexes among them. Because all the environments permit of crop growing and animal husbandry, they all show an intensive modern development in which nineteenth- and twentieth-century water control systems are fairly well developed, both for flood control and for irrigation. Because many of the mainland core regions are threaded by rivers that are navigable for small craft in the lower reaches of the rivers and because road building presents difficulties in wet lowlands, there are again similarities. Since these regional cores range from desert patterns of Pakistan's Indus River Valley to South Vietnam's tropical Mekong Delta and to northernmost China's winterbound Ussuri Valley, there are some strong regional contrasts in the seasonal and cyclic correlative conditions that go with river valleys. Within the island realms there is a general similarity in broad pattern but a variety in detail. Habits of living vary from regional environment to environment, and the cultural imprints upon the physical bases vary markedly.

The uplands that basically form the bounding limits to the varied regional environments also vary markedly, both in their physical makeup and in the efficiency with which they separate the regional cores. The multiple ranges separating India and China perhaps have been the most effective regional barrier of all, but this is almost a special case. For example, although the separations between Burma and Thailand have been historically of such significance that Burmese and Thai cultures are clearly different, the barrier has often been breached by militant operations of one or the other culture group. Within India and China both internal physical barriers and zones of separation have been such that early cultures showed considerable regional variation. These regional patterns have produced regionally separated languages, habituated daily customs, and political separatisms, in historic terms. However, in the long run none of the internal physical separations, barriers, or divides within either India or China has been very effective at holding apart warring elements, processes of cultural diffusion, or interregional trading operations. Human persistence and organizational skills have transcended all such internal barriers throughout much of the historic period in both large physical regions. Within the island sector the wide scattering of islands presented many separated local environments during earlier eras of simpler technology, permitting many local regionalisms. However, the development of effective water transport systems slowly provided the linkage system that could bring separate island groups within the frameworks of larger regional orbits by the initiative of some one culture group operating on the coastal seas.

The summary impression, therefore, for the whole of the Orient is that there exist physical bounds that divide the realm into fifty to sixty separate "regions" in which early ethnic groups could develop separate culture systems. Simple technologies prevented widespread organizational structures of economic and political varieties, and these early culture groups did develop cultural individualisms that have persisted into modern time. However, the growing systems of technology abetted human tendencies to ignore the bounds of physical environments so that no regional culture system has historically evolved without cultural contamination from neighboring or distant culture systems. To the end that Indian and Chinese societies spread their influences widely, those two culture systems bridged the barrier and linked the various regions with numerous common denominator culture elements. It is in Southeast Asia that the greatest of the intermixing of the two dominant cultures was greatest, the very zone in which the physical bounds suggest, at least, that regional cultural distinction might be greatest.

Kinds of Landscapes

If you followed upon the implications of the preceding section, you would think that landscapes could obviously be separated into those of the mountains, plains, hilly patches, small islands, or deltaic swamps. Such is not the present intention. The concern is rather for the kinds of cultivated landscapes that have been created as people have lived in and utilized various resources of portions of the Orient and for the visual appearance of the open countryside (Fig. 8). No attempt is made to carry this picture building down to the localized level in a way that will describe every small local region.

The single most common kind of landscape is that of the wet-rice field, one to be found in every country in the Orient as a major element in the total landscape. There is a considerable seasonal variety in the mien of the wet-rice field landscape, but the most notable and distinctive aspect is that of late spring-early summer. At that season the wide spread of the watery surface flashes reflections of light, clouds, and perhaps nearby trees from its liquid veneer, broken into small facets by the irregular lines of the bunds or field divisions. The young rice has not yet grown so tall that it obscures the watery reflective element. Seasonally, this aspect is followed by the greening of the landscape as the rice grows tall and then the yellowing as the rice ripens. Next comes the landscape of dull yellows and browns of the ripe fields or perhaps of harvested fields now showing stubble, but this is likely to be a landscape full of people in bright clothing busily at work on the harvest. The post-harvest landscape darkens to dull browns, reds, and blacks of the varied soil patterns as the imprint of the previous crop weakens and the fields are plowed in preparation for the next crop of rice.

In northern Japan this cyclic transformation of the rice field landscape occurs but once a year, but in selected areas where there adequate water and mild climate the transformation may occur twice a year, and in a few localities three times a year. The annual shift in appearance is the more common, for most farmers prefer the long-season rices that require seven to eight months of field occupance. There are many sub-types of the wet-rice field landscape. On valley floors and coastal plains of low gradient the fields tend to be larger, the bunds seem insignificant, the landscape appears flat and monotonous, and one may feel isolated in a sea of rice fields. As the relief of the land sharpens, the bunds stand out in greater prominence, and the higher backwall of a terraced field is capped by the water-retaining bund. According to the strength of the relief and its local intricacy the terraced wet-rice field landscape becomes an intricately etched mosaic of odd bits and pieces in bewildering irregularity, but also of precise and ordered dimensions, for all fields must be level and the sculpting of fields out of hill surfaces is done on the contour.

Valley bottom rice-field landscapes having high water tables do not often abound in trees, but then there sometimes is the fitting of the rice-fields to the very lowest lands, with trees occupying the higher parts, often no more than two or three feet above the wet field levels. In some areas the wet-rice landscape is almost a closed landscape as patches of tall coconut trees and lower shrubby fruiting trees alternate, closing off the long view. In other areas treescapes are absent and the rice fields stretch for miles. In the lower and deltaic zones there is seasonal contrast according to the local flood season so that in summer the watery land-scape stretches away, with rivers, ponds, marshy tracts, and swamp rice zones all full and high in level. Sometimes the extra heavy rainy season brings water to the very dike tops, or even over them, and a lowland landscape becomes an inland sea. In the winter periods, on the other hand, water levels recede, lakes shrink, rivers withdraw into their chan-nels, and the reds, browns, and blacks of foreshores, dike lines, field bunds, and road embankments stand out.

Around the irregularly delimited margins of the valley bottoms there usually is more local variety in the landscape, as the rice landscape pene-trates the upland along the tributary valleys, alternating with the terraced valley margins and the upland zones of irregularly arranged fields having scattered to heavy tree covers. Most of the lower hill country throughout the Orient has been taken into the cultivated landscape system to some degree. In some areas permanent dry-field systems have been installed, reducing the treescapes somewhat, but in other areas not yet under the heaviest pressures the land use is that of irregular shifting cultivation that creates erratic marks and a variety of successional patterns over the hilly country. In areas of long and steady occupation the hilly margins surrounding the plains often have been terraced into acutely sculptured mosaics that resemble garden systems rather than the broad fields of crop land that the occidental associates with agriculture. These may be wet-field patches where water is available alternating with sections of dry-field lands set with trees along terrace margins and growing a variety of crop plants. In some areas, such as central Japan and southeastern China, the dry-field hillscapes are planted in tea, the pruning-plucking tending to add to the visual sense of contoured and sculptured terrace systems.

The wet-rice field landscape often penetrates well into the higher hill country, and vistas of terraced wet fields occur at varied levels. Along the Himalayan front of northern India, in the Indonesian and Philippine highlands, in the southern Japanese islands, in central to southern Korea, in central and western China, and in some of the plateau units of penin-sular Southeast Asia the terraced wet-rice field landscape becomes an important element in the total cultivated landscape at elevations well above 5,000 feet.

Since rice yields higher volumes of the basic staple food product than do other grains, the wet-rice field landscape has been steadily invading the dry margins of portions of the Orient in the modern period as irriga-tion facilities extend the availability of water supplies. Thus, today, the wet-rice field landscape is part of the total landscape in the Indus Valley of Pakistan. To a lesser extent the wet-rice field landscape has moved

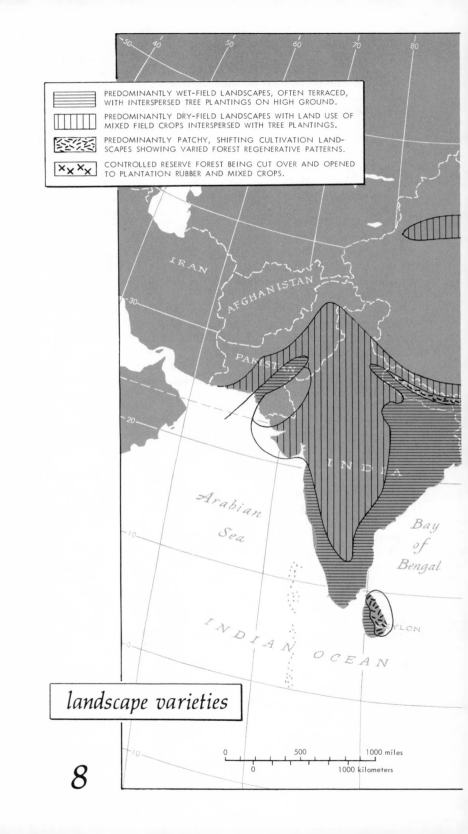

PREDOMINANTLY WET-FIELD LANDSCAPES, OFTEN TERRACED, WITH INTERSPERSED TREE PLANTINGS ON HIGH GROUND.

PREDOMINANTLY DRY-FIELD LANDSCAPES WITH LAND USE OF MIXED FIELD CROPS INTERSPERSED WITH TREE PLANTINGS.

PREDOMINANTLY PATCHY, SHIFTING CULTIVATION LAND-SCAPES SHOWING VARIED FOREST REGENERATIVE PATTERNS.

CONTROLLED RESERVE FOREST BEING CUT OVER AND OPENED TO PLANTATION RUBBER AND MIXED CROPS.

IRAN

AFGHANISTAN

PAKISTAN

INDIA

Arabian Sea

Bay of Bengal

INDIAN OCEAN

CEYLON

landscape varieties

| 0 | | 500 | | 1000 miles |

| 0 | | 1000 kilometers |

8

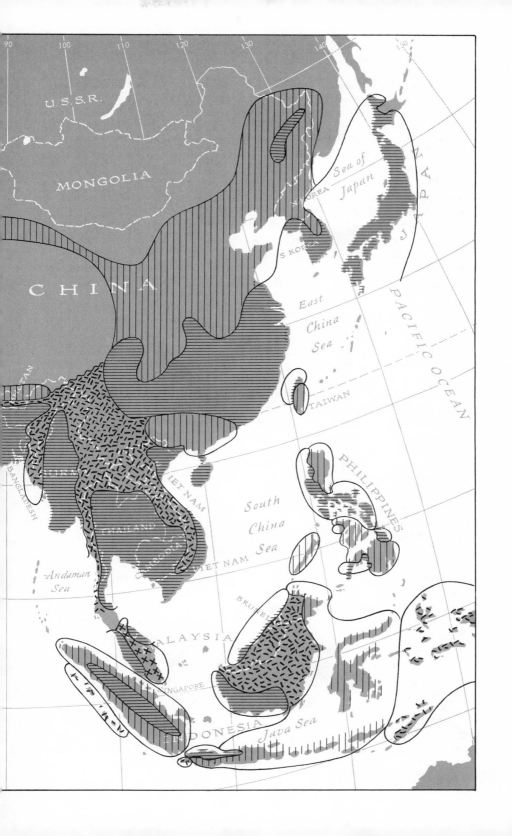

northwestward in China. Steadily progressing against the dry-field land-scapes of other portions of the Orient, the wet-rice field landscape has grown over the centuries to its premier position. There is little of the old and intricately sculpted terracing being installed throughout the Orient today, but in zones in which old dry-field lands are amenable to the application of water the wet-field landscape still is growing in extent and relative dominance.

Throughout most portions of the Orient there remains a dry-field crop landscape composed of various elements. This dry-field pattern is not extensive today in the peninsular portions of mainland Southeast Asia, but it becomes the dominant element in the drier parts of India, Pakistan, northern China, northern Korea, and central to northern Japan. Although traditional field patterns are normally smaller than in the American scene, the dry-field landscape is a more familiar one, with field appearances that are similar in that wheat, barley, sorghum, beans, peas, and similar crops show up. Winter wheat landscapes of northern China resemble those of portions of the Occident. The farm landscapes of northernmost Honshu and most of Hokkaido bear resemblances to those of the American upper midwest.

This dry-field landscape often mixes crop plants of the Occident and those of the Orient, in that the "cotton belt" of China lies chiefly within the "wheat belt," and soy beans and corn are to be found in common association in field patterns. This is not as distinctive a kind of landscape as that of the wet-rice field landscape because crop plants are more mixed, field patterns bear resemblance to those found in other parts of the earth, and cultivation practices are roughly similar. This is particu-larly true in some of the areas in which modern mechanization has been brought to bear on agricultural production, enlarging the field patterns to those familiar to the occidental.

There are other landscapes that are more distinctive to the Orient. The coconut landscape of much of the southern half of the Philippines, the west coastal fringe of West Malaysia, portions of the west Indian coast, the southeastern coast of Ceylon, and coastal sections of many Indonesian islands is a significantly distinctive one. Chiefly a closed landscape of short vistas through myriads of bare tree trunks, the tall structure of the mature coconut landscape creates a vista that is equalled nowhere in the Occident. It is a landscape that is always predominantly dull green that does not have significant seasonal changes in appearance, and that more resembles a strange kind of forest country than farmscape. Even more like forest country is the rubber-tree landscape in the "spring" wet season. Monotonously green and uniform in appearance the rubber landscapes of west central West Malaysia stretch for miles upon miles, punctuated only by patches of replanting of new varieties into the older stocks. As grown on the plantation lands in portions of southern India, western Ceylon, much of Sumatra, and in both West and East Malaysia the rubber landscape has been growing more extensive with each passing decade during the twentieth century. The rubber tree is not particularly beautiful or distinctive in appearance, as is the tall coconut palm, and when massed by the millions the visual impact is one of dulling monotony. The older and traditional planting systems of the Orient mixed many things together in jungle-like heterogeneity and spatial proximity, giving a never-ending variety to the cultivated landscape that is missing in the modern moncrop cultivated landscape of large fields and geometrically spaced plantings.

Within the southern sector of the oriental world, south of China, the landscapes of the jungle and forest in many localities still obtrude aspects of the wild, untamed, unrestrainable, and overwhelming profusion of vegetation that blankets the surface of the earth. This cover once was very extensive in its wild state, and nature tends to reassert itself profusely in any areas in which man once reduced the region to cultivated state but then relaxed his efforts at control. Cambodia is the classic illustration of this resurgence of forest in the wake of the declining Khmer Empire of the fifteenth century, to the end that in the nineteenth century the wonders of Angkor were "discovered" among the forests of western Cambodia, but the many early marks of Indian contact in Sumatra, West Malaysia, and Borneo have been fairly thoroughly obliterated. In the modern era the wild jungle and forest aspect is in retreat, however, as the cultivated landscapes inexorably expand against the jungle-forest in the face of seemingly continuous population growth. In most sectors of the Orient today, the timber loggers often precede the cultivators to cull out the merchantable timber and opening the roads, routes, and trails as lines of settlement access. In many regions, however, the shifting cultivator has long preceded both the logger and the sedentary farmer so that many of the upland forested landscapes show the pockmarking imprint of successional vegetative patterns that go with periodic shifting cultivation. New clearings, thick, young jungle growth, immature forest patches, and old forest remnants often alternate in jigsaw puzzle patterns, although in some regions grassland successions often delay the return of the forest cover.

There must be at least 1,500,000 villages in the Orient, in which the great majority of the populace lives, and the village landscapes of the Orient are both distinctive and show regional variation. It is only recently that wheeled vehicle transport has provided access to most villages, with the modern programs of road building. Villages are located everywhere from delta fringes to mountain heights, and their variety in appearance is great, but certain patterns do stand out, for some village landscapes are both distinctive and do show regional variation. The village of the North China Plain, in northern China, tends to be a tightly clustered affair, dull brown to gray in appearance, utilitarian and seldom showing decorative elements, often aligned along only one or two streets. Its houses most often are heavily built of adobe, set on a low platform on the ground, with medium-pitched roofs of thatch or gray tile. The village is set in crop fields that come close against its perimeter. Threshing floors and storage bins are inside the village. A thin and scrubby cover of trees shows up in scattered distribution. The Malay village of West Malaysia, on the other hand, is a straggly affair aligned along a watercourse, almost totally hidden behind and under a luxuriant cover of trees and shrubs. Houses are usually built of wood, and each is in its own cluster of trees and shrubs and is set apart from its neighbors. Malay houses are set on pilings, well off the ground, with space beneath utilized for storage.

The Yangtze Valley villages tend to be linear affairs placed along river banks, often on dike tops, extending a half mile or more. Housing tends to be flimsily built of bamboo-matting-thatch, set on the ground, although an old and long-established village may well have some houses with plastered walls covering bamboo panels. Planting often is scant and houses are set close together. The Indian village of the upper Ganges Valley in northern India also tends to be a tightly clustered affairs, set on a low mound that is the accumulation of centuries. Housing is tightly built, often of adobe and with flat roofs, substantial appearing but not really permanent in nature, and often using party-walls so that living units are in close proximity, and alleys and lanes give variable access to the interior. Such villages are often surrounded by semi-open spaces in which clumps of trees, shrubs, straw stacks, animal bedding grounds, heaps of animal dung kept for domestic fuel, and cart and tool storage spots indiscriminately are jumbled together between the crop fields and the houses.

Although the landscape of China does show some regional variation in types of houses and architectural styles, there is broad uniformity in basic elements (Fig. 9). Indian-Pakistan, on the other hand, shows a bewildering variety of types of houses. Some of these appear to relate to environmental factors, but others obviously are culturally derived and must relate to ethnic diversity and cultural variation. Notable in the Chinese village landscape is the simplicity of pattern from one end of a village to the other, economic and social status being marked only by the size of the house unit, or the numbers of units, occupied by any one family. Quite visible to the alien visitor to India, on the other hand, is the social segregation of different status groups in particular parts of a village when that village contains more than one social stratum.

Villages in Burma, Thailand, Cambodia, the Philippines, and Indonesia tend to somewhat resemble those of Malaysia in that they normally are set in copious plantings of trees and shrubs, are not conspicuous on the landscape, and provide relative privacy to their occupants. Vietnamese villages tend to resemble the Chinese patterns in the broad sense. Korean villages tend to be small clusters of houses recessed into some landform irregularity, but not separated from each other by tree and shrub plantings. Their traditional style of building on a platform on the ground, their heavily thatched roofs with very wide overhangs, their housing units arranged around a courtyard-threshing floor are perhaps the most distinctive appearing of all oriental village styles. Japanese villages traditionally tended to be straggly affairs along a path system, with highly varied local styles of finishing off a wood-and-thatch architecture. But Japanese villages are perhaps modernizing more rapidly than those of any portion of the Orient, and traditional architecture is disappearing. Single-story and two-story housing built in wood, with many windows, roofed by brightly colored metal tiles are rapidly transforming the appearance of the Japanese village landscape. The straggly scattering of houses continues, but roads replace paths, and the forest of TV antennas replaces the tree growth of the former era.

There are parts of the Orient in which one finds mixtures in regional landscapes that can be identified. For example, the traveler in Malaysia can soon learn to determine from the rural landscape the ethnic elements that are regionally dominant. The Chinese village or small town shows a great many basic and secondary characteristics that clearly denote its ethnic mix, as opposed to the Malay village or small town. This also shows up on the open countryside when one comes upon a Chinese temple or a Moslem mosque. The Chinese agriculturist, though not as neat as a Japanese, demonstrates in his handling of the landscape that he is at heart much more the farmer than is demonstrated by the Malay.

There is a certain air of disorderly scattering of things in a rural India landscape that normally is quite absent in the Japanese landscape with its closely tailored and even prim orderliness. The Koreal rural landscape has about it a certain casual air that is different from the casualness that is seen in the Philippine landscape; the former gives the impression of simply not trying to be precise and totally efficient, and the latter suggests an attitude of never quite being able to cope with nature and not really trying to do so.

There is another intangible element of variation in the landscape. Since the Chinese have seldom tried to build for perpetuity, there really are few features, remnants, or artifacts of the far past still to be seen in the Chinese landscape. Shrines, objects of local worship, elements of monumental intent are present in the Chinese landscape, but once they have become run down, neglected, or discarded, their artifactual evidence disappears rather rapidly—perhaps to be used in other construction at a different site. The Indian landscape, on the other hand, abounds in elements out of the past, and monuments, symbolic constructs, or ruins in variable state of disarray or disassembly are to be seen in many localities and add to the irregular disorderliness of the Indian landscape.

Related to the monumental architecture of the past, of course, is the monumental architecture of the present, expressed in temples, shrines, formal parks and gardens, monuments to historic incidents, and to lesser degree in the carry over of design motifs into public architecture. Although these elements are less conspicuous today when occidental architectures have invaded the Orient, and although such elements relate largely to the urban zones, Japaneseness, Chineseness, or Malayness imparts its characteristic imprint to the traveler.

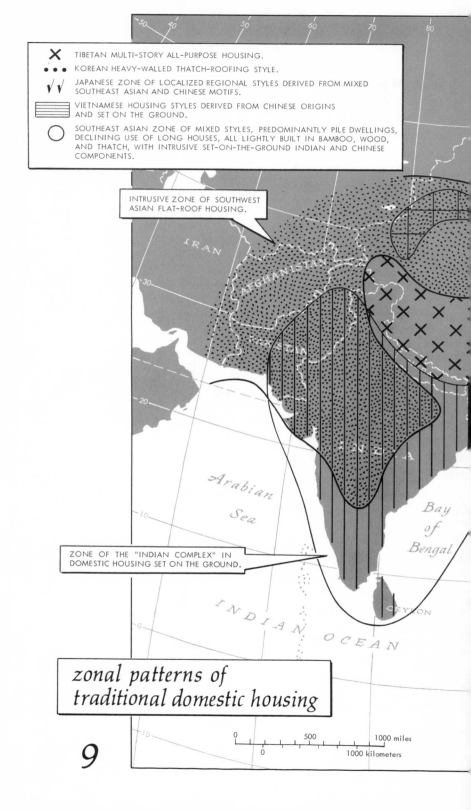

TIBETAN MULTI-STORY ALL-PURPOSE HOUSING.

KOREAN HEAVY-WALLED THATCH-ROOFING STYLE.

JAPANESE ZONE OF LOCALIZED REGIONAL STYLES DERIVED FROM MIXED SOUTHEAST ASIAN AND CHINESE MOTIFS.

VIETNAMESE HOUSING STYLES DERIVED FROM CHINESE ORIGINS AND SET ON THE GROUND.

SOUTHEAST ASIAN ZONE OF MIXED STYLES, PREDOMINANTLY PILE DWELLINGS, DECLINING USE OF LONG HOUSES, ALL LIGHTLY BUILT IN BAMBOO, WOOD, AND THATCH, WITH INTRUSIVE SET-ON-THE-GROUND INDIAN AND CHINESE COMPONENTS.

INTRUSIVE ZONE OF SOUTHWEST ASIAN FLAT-ROOF HOUSING.

ZONE OF THE "INDIAN COMPLEX" IN DOMESTIC HOUSING SET ON THE GROUND.

zonal patterns of traditional domestic housing

9

peoples,
and too many people

The Orient, or the oriental world, contains no strange and peculiar human types by which to explain it in genetic terms alone, for that world contains elements of almost all the primary racial strains of the earth in some percentage. These range from solid population blocks of rather high uniformity to very small remnantal groups composed of a particular ethnic strain, and to regional populations in which the degree of inter-mixture clearly indicates wide genetic inheritance. The largest numbers of people, of course, do derive from the Mongoloid ethnic incubator, early or late, accounting for the largest components everywhere except in the Indian subcontinent and in New Guinea. No discussion of ethnic com-position for the oriental world can effectively begin with Peking Man or Java Man, and these pages attempt only a crude approximation of the ethnic origins and relative compositions for the populations now resident in the several societies of the Orient. The very nature of environments has been altered too greatly since the time of Peking Man, and our paleobiological record is too thin to permit real continuity in our dis-cussion. Such elements involve the Pleistocene building of the Loess Highlands of northwest China, the growth of the North China Plain, the drowning of the coastal fringes of eastern Asia, and the proliferation of island archipelagoes through the rise of sea level to its present general stand. Particular portions of the oriental world have probably been among the more populous regions of the earth ever since man achieved his position of biologic dominance among the life forms of the earth, and "China" and "India" have probably been world population leaders for much of the historic period. That headstart is, in a sense, now reaping the whirlwind of regional overpopulation for both China and India. There are other regions within the oriental world, however, that have become almost too heavily populated within recent centuries, and one of the chief difficulties that man faces in the oriental world is that there are just too many people, everywhere.

Human Origins and Ethnic Identities

Whether they derive from Africa, solely, or evolved as a widely spread Old World tropical strain, the Congoid peoples of dark skins and curly hair are represented only in the southern fringes of the oriental world (Fig. 10). The dark skin pigmentation is strongest in the Indian subcontinent, but it is also present in mainland southeastern Asia, in the island world generally but clearly in New Guinea. At an earlier date the Congoid percentage of the then population was greater than it has been in the last millennium for, except for New Guinea, the Congoid element is a receding one as population growth derives from other racial strains. Congoid elements apparently never penetrated far into mainland Asia, northern India and southern China being their most northern extents. In the contemporary era, of course, the black members of the United States military forces have introduced Congoid genetic elements into the populations of all of eastern Asia, from Japan to southern Vietnam, to renew their minor element in the population mix.

From a southwestern Asian racial incubator Caucasoid strains have been introduced into the oriental world from a very early date. In one directional component this has taken the form of immigrations into India, and far eastward into New Guinea at the very least, although the numbers moving beyond India have probably not been very great. The invasions of India in the prehistoric and historic periods have been sufficiently strong to dominate the genetic inheritance of modern Indian populations, particularly those of northern India-Pakistan. The other directional component of Caucasoid immigration into the Oriental world moved via Central Asia, where there has been long intermixture between Mongoloid and Caucasoid strains. Marginal small streams of Caucasoid migrants must have penetrated eastern Asia at an early date, the most distant of these reaching Japan and giving rise to the Ainu aboriginal stock of the Japanese islands. Since the Columbian Discoveries, of course, Caucasoid elements from the European world have entered into the genetic inheritance of all parts of the oriental world in some small percentage element. This has taken the form of Spanish and white-American genetic intrusion into the Philippines, British intrusion into India-Pakistan-Ceylon-Burma, French intrusion into Vietnam, and Dutch intrusion into Indonesia. Such regions as Thailand, China, Korea, and Japan show small elements from all parts of the occidental world in the contemporary period.

The Mongoloid racial incubator of northwest China-Mongolia, perhaps the latest of the three main operative human hearths of the Old World, has turned out a great many broods of people, each a little different in genetic construct over the long period (see Fig. 10). In terms of numbers, the primary directional components of movement for Mongoloid peoples have been toward the southeast. Westward components of movement, of course, took groups westward toward Europe, into Tibet, northward into Siberia (and across into the New World), and eastward

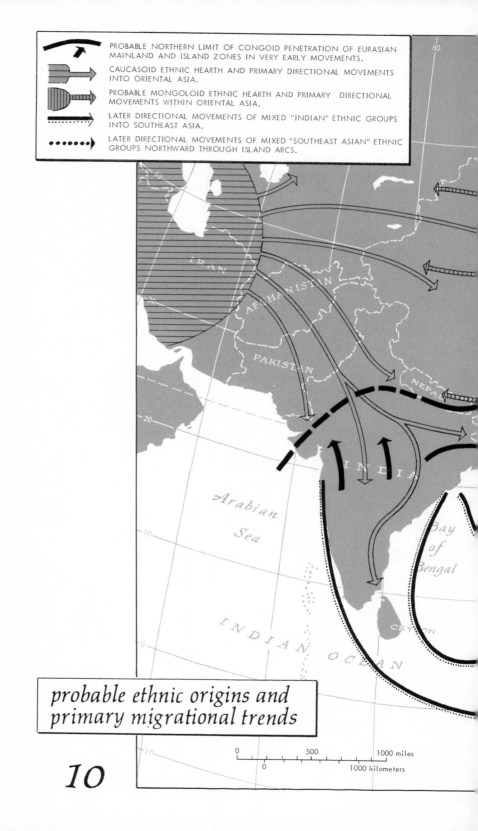

PROBABLE NORTHERN LIMIT OF CONGOID PENETRATION OF EURASIAN MAINLAND AND ISLAND ZONES IN VERY EARLY MOVEMENTS.

CAUCASOID ETHNIC HEARTH AND PRIMARY DIRECTIONAL MOVEMENTS INTO ORIENTAL ASIA.

PROBABLE MONGOLOID ETHNIC HEARTH AND PRIMARY DIRECTIONAL MOVEMENTS WITHIN ORIENTAL ASIA.

LATER DIRECTIONAL MOVEMENTS OF MIXED "INDIAN" ETHNIC GROUPS INTO SOUTHEAST ASIA.

LATER DIRECTIONAL MOVEMENTS OF MIXED "SOUTHEAST ASIAN" ETHNIC GROUPS NORTHWARD THROUGH ISLAND ARCS.

probable ethnic origins and primary migrational trends

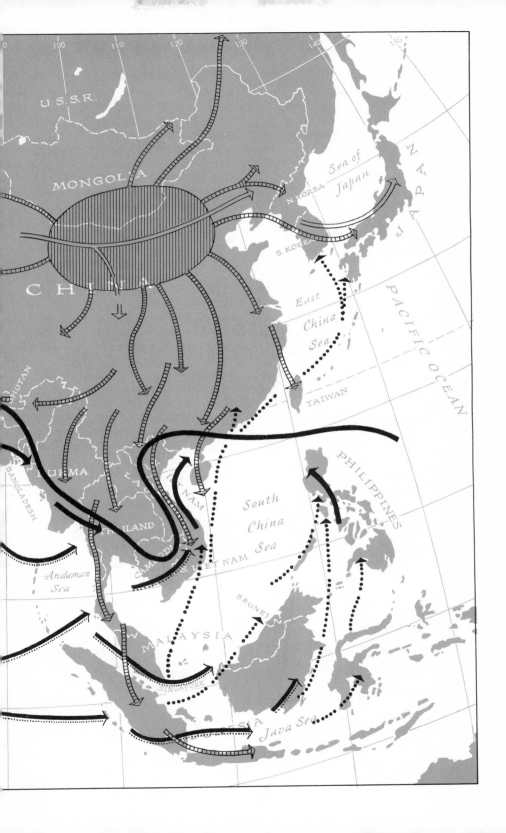

into Korea and Japan. In the southeasterly drift, early Mongoloid peoples moved into all the lands of mainland southeast Asia and into the island world beyond, small elements setting forth into the Pacific toward the islands of the open ocean. During the historic period, it has been the North China segment of the Mongoloid hearth that has provided the emigrant broods, as the Chinese drifted southward within China, exerting pressures on earlier emigrants to the end that many of them migrated farther southward into the peninsular corner of the continent, into what today we label Burma, Thailand, Malaysia, Cambodia, Laos, and Vietnam. This southward drift has continued right into the contemporary era, as nonChinese tribal peoples move southward out of China, and as Chinese from southern China have migrated southward into Vietnam, Thailand, Malaysia, Indonesia, and across to the Philippines.

In the twentieth century there has also been a northward movement of Chinese, as northern Chinese have populated Manchuria and converted the former pastoral ranges into sedentary farmscapes. Recurrent short-term movements have punctuated the history of China for at least two millennia, as agricultural settlers spread into the open grasslands of Inner Mongolia and into Chinese Central Asia during humid periods or intervals of Chinese political strength and then withdrew during either climatically dry periods or periods of Chinese political weakness.

The three sources for three primary racial strains have provided the basic settlement patterns and the modern genetic inheritances for the peoples of the oriental world. However, there have been many cross-current and countermovement elements that account for the particular ethnic constructs of the large regions, the specific environments, and the political states of the present system. An apparently recurrent element of northward movement along the coastal fringe and the island arcs apparently took streams of southern peoples out of some sector of southeastern Asia (Vietnam to Java?) along the China coast and through the Philippines-Ryukyu arcs into southern Korea and southernmost Japan at some date well before the onset of the Christian Era (see Fig. 10). Median-interval streams of such movements brought small early populations into the Philippines, and later streams out of Indonesia introduced the large ethnic components of the modern Philippines. The Cham element of Vietnam appears to be related to the early northward flow from a southern source, contributing to the ethnic mix of Vietnam. Apparently, various ethnic stocks of uncertain basic origin that mixed into the Congoid elements of peninsular southeastern Asia moved out of India at a very early date and provided the earliest regional populations of Mons, Khmers, and other groups not now identifiable in the several regional units of the peninsular zone. The later southward drift of such groups as the Burmese, Karens, Shans, Kachins, Thai, and Vietnamese cut across the grain of that earlier easterly flow, following down the linear trends of the physiographic structure of mainland southeastern Asia and separating into the several regional homelands that they now occupy.

Both North and South Vietnam have a political boundary that includes considerable mountain country along their western flanks into which migrant groups have been moving out of China for centuries. There are numerous disjunct ethnic stocks, some of them scattered at altitudinal levels by habituated living systems, almost all of which have little in common with any variety of Vietnamese. The Vietnamese are lowlanders of long habit with well-defined agricultural systems and who originated in southernmost China and have been moving southward since before the start of the Christian Era until they now dominate the long coastal lawland of Vietnam.

Cambodia, the old heartland of the Khmer Empire, holds a modern residue of the Khmer peoples, with a population now growing again. Its hilly margins also are home to a number of disjunct ethnic stocks of rather wide variation, and within its western political margins live some Thai. Vietnamese have been moving into Cambodia in the last century, out of the Mekong Delta, to create an ethnic pluralism.

Thailand, centering on the Menam Chao Phraya, was a tributary region under the Khmer Empire which contained small colonies of Khmer and Mon peoples. The Thai began migrating southward out of China in the tenth century, following the Chao Phraya southward to its delta and spreading out to the east and west on the river plain. The hilly margins of western Thailand are home to numerous other groups out of China, for example, the Karen, Palaung, and Shan, and to the north the hill country contains several Miao ethnic stocks relatively recently derived from China. A few Khmer have long continued to live within the Thai boundary against Cambodia, and in the far south Malays occupy the southernmost peninsular margins, against Malaysia. In national policy, the Thai pretend to ignore these elements of ethnic pluralism in favor of an attitude of unanimity.

Burma remains one of the lands of mixed ethnic stocks in which the ethnic element makes for cultural and political instability. Burmans (the tribal ethnic-stock name, from which the terms Burma and Burmese derive) out of southwest China were the first to reach the Irrawabby lowlands, among the emigrants from China, submerging the Mon and other India-derived ethnic elements of the lower valley country. The Burmans were followed by the Karen, Shan, Palaung, and Kachin, all of whom have regional upland homes to the north and east, and by other small ethnic groups that remain in the northern hilly margins. The Chin of the western hill country of Burma and the Naga of the northwest may well represent the earliest of the Mongoloid migrants out of the corner of China, but there have been varied mixtures into Indian ethnic stocks over a long period, and their fractionation into divergent language groupings makes their placement difficult. The Burmans inherited the best regional homeland in the lowlands and have so increased in relative numbers in comparison with other ethnic groups that they now dominate the country.

Laos, a political state only on modern political maps and a modern creation of French colonialism, is a region of mainland southeastern Asia without a lowland core, and its fractionated and disjunct ethnic mix reflects clearly the failure of coherence of a culture group around and in a lowland regional setting. Its most numerous element, called Lao, is closely related to the Thai and were migrants out of China at about the same time. Some of the lesser ethnic elements may have preceded the

Lao, but numerous groups have come more recently and have found fragmented homelands in the higher hill country.

West Malaysia apparently was a zone of passage to the earliest migrating human groups, but small stocks of pre-Malay peoples were widely scattered as the Malays came into and through the peninsula. Various Malay groupings scattered out over the peninsula in preferred riverine localities to form the progenitors of the modern Malay population. Port villages and towns were long the landfall-calling points for seamen from many countries. In the modern period Chinese and Indians were invited into Malaya by British colonial control, as economically productive elements, so that modern West Malaysia has developed a three-part ethnic structure.

Western Indonesia apparently held a variety of small ethnic groups prior to the primary Malay immigrant population arrived. It is very unclear how much genetic intrusion came out of Indian historic contacts around the start of the Christian Era, and it is equally unclear whether or not very much actual genetic intrusion surrounded the Islamization of Indonesia in the fifteenth century, but Indonesia does have a mixed ancestry in terms of the long past. Since 1800, when the modern Indonesian population began its dramatic growth spurt, there has not been great genetic intermixture so that the contemporary Indonesian population represents a modern native blend of very early mixed origins, regionally separated into many substocks.

The Philippines seem to have been populated at one time by a very widely scattered population of Negritoes at a low-density level, for there were widely scattered remnants of Negritoes in the sixteenth century. Also widely scattered are elements of a racial strain often labeled proto-Malay, but such distinctions largely are cultural rather than biologic. The primary Philippine population is Malay, derived from long-continued migratory movements of peoples out of western Indonesia or the southernmost mainland portions of Southeast Asia. Since the fifteenth century, however, there have been small percentage additions to the Philippine ethnic mix from many sources. Chinese, Spanish, varied other European elements and, since 1900, diverse ethnic elements from the United States have been added. The Spanish element is less than often presumed, and the Chinese element is greater than often admitted. Statistics on Chinese intermarriage have never been adequately kept, many Chinese have Philippinized their names, and the share of Chinese blood in the modern Philippines could be as high as 10%.

Japan today is the oriental country most uniform in its ethnic structure, but its early background is a very mixed one. The Caucasoid Ainu may form the aboriginal element contributing to the modern population. Whether the influx of peoples from the far south came next or whether mainland Mongolic elements via Korea were next, these latter two became blended together in the very early centuries of the Christian Era, with the addition of a small percentage of Korean and the absorption of a share of the Ainu, to produce an early mixed stock of Japanese. The modern Japanese have expanded out of this early mixed blend with but little genetic intrusion from other ethnic stocks until the contemporary period.

Korea is probably the second most uniform country in the oriental world, in ethnic terms, though it is not entirely clear as to what the origin of the Koreans may be. They are probably mixed Tungusic Mongoloid for the most part, with a little Chinese blood and some feedback additions of genetic elements out of southern Japan at an early point. Historically, the Korean population derives from this early mix, expanding upon its own base until the twentieth century, at which point various minor genetic elements are being added. In historic terms there never has been strong distinction between a northern and southern Korean ethnic strain, and the line between North Korea and South Korea is more climatically than ethnically important, but a clear separation of the two halves of the original country for a long period of time could begin to develop aspects of genetic separation.

China, as a country or a political state, has never represented a discrete ethnic entity, for the controlling element in "Chineseness" is not primarily genetic, but cultural. Whoever thinks Chinese and adopts Chinese customs may become a Chinese in the full sense of the term. Therefore, the Chinese, genetically, include various and divergent biologic elements. The Chinese, of course, are primarily Mongoloid in the broad sense of the primary racial strain, but there are Chinese akin to the Vietnamese, Thai, and Shan on the one geographical frontier, to Koreans and Mongols on another, and to various Turkic peoples on the western frontier. Many kinds of precise ethnic strains, all culturally "barbarians" to the Chinese, have over the long term accepted Chinese ways and have become merged into the broad genetic structure of the Chinese. Many cultural groups, on the other hand, closely related in ethnic and genetic terms, have refused to become Chinese in cultural terms and, thus, remain "barbarian," non-Chinese, and "minority" elements within the Chinese state. These non-Chinese elements are strongest in south and southwest China, in Tibet, and in Chinese Central Asia. The latter region, of course, includes many Turkic intermixtures of Mongoloid-Caucasoid racial strains.

Chinese society never has been structured in such a way that, among Chinese themselves, variations in ethnic origins or relationships were very significant. Regionalisms there always have been, and in historic terms these have taken the shape of political regionalisms, since political territorialism increasingly conformed to geographic regionalisms. Shansi Chinese do appear superficially different from Kwangtung Chinese in skin pigmentation and body build, and they speak different languages (though they read and write the same language), but though both recognize that there are differences in the two cultural psychologies, they are both united in being essentially Chinese in the important cultural criteria. In this respect China is one society and it is not intrinsically torn by ethnic pluralisms that so strongly bother Malaysia, Burma, or India.

India-Pakistan-Bangladesh-Ceylon as a unit forms the one large portion of the oriental world that does not contain significant Mongoloid ethnic components. The margins of the Mongoloid zone lie along the Himalayas in the north and along the ranges of the Burma-India border in the east, although a small and very old ethnic intrusion of Mongoloid blood seeped down into the Assam Valley and into the Assam Plateau. Nepal, Sikkim, and Bhutan chiefly contain Indian ethnic strains out of the lowlands, but there is a Mongoloid component in all the Himalayan mountain country from the Hindu Kush to Burma. It is in the Indian subcontinent that the largest problems in ethnic relationships lie. There were obvious Congoid elements in a very early peopling of the peninsular zone, for there have been sufficient remnants of Negrito and full-statured prototypes to support the supposition that southern India once held such a population. The ethnic strains that go with the Dravidian languages, however, represent a puzzle as to genetic racial origins. Commonly called Australoid, do such remnants represent a very old eastern Congoid pre-black stock or do they represent the product of a localized racial hearth? Whatever the precise origins of the dark-pigmented racial stocks, they form a significant substructure to the peninsular population pyramid.

North Indian populations at least as far back as the Indus Valley civilizations, depicted at Mohenjo-daro, seem to bear relationships to the peoples to the west at least as far as the Tigris-Euphrates river country, and they probably represent close to the earliest products of the Caucasoid racial incubator. All later immigrants into India from the northwest came out of this same racial hearth, represented by varied historic strains. The historiography of northern India suggests that the Indo-Aryan invasions brought in peoples of lighter skin pigmentation and that a color line early became a matter of social distinction in northern India, but skin pigmentation is the only ethnic element than can be read out of that record. Historic invasions of India, including the late Islamic ones, brought a large volume of light skin pigmentation into India from the late Caucasoid hearth. Historic invasions of India have penetrated deeply, both to the east and to the south, interlayering the darker-skinned elements, to the end that India has become quite mixed (see Fig. 10). The multiple social stratifications of modern India have added complication to the ethnic problem. Although many ascribe racial significance to caste evolution, there is an essential cultural factoring normally involved. Marriage within caste lines does perpetuate genetic inheritance, but the complicated evolution of modern Indian caste structures does not permit simple generalizations of value as to genetic inheritance. India-Pakistan-Bangladesh-Ceylon today possesses a mixed genetic background in which both light and dark skin pigmentations, various blood groupings, a wide range of long-short headedness, and several other biologic aspects are present in very mixed assemblages. It seems clear that the Mongoloid racial strains are not significant and that the Indian subcontinent's racial origins lie with the Congoid and Caucasoid racial hearths, with the preponderance of racial characteristics from the latter, but more than this is hard to state.

For the modern political states on the Indian subcontinent there is no separable generalization, since all are involved historically in the mixed patterns. For all political states operative in 1972, the concept of the social community has far more validity than to attempt to take things apart on racial terms. But even here one sees that all are mixed. Social community separations are strong with Ceylon; in India social community aspects become bewilderingly complex, as they also do in the border zones of Pakistan. Bangladesh, by its recent separation from Pakistan, is slightly more unified than the others, but here community issues rankle at the local level still. In all four areas issues of language have entered into the socio-ethnic question in the modern period as factors in maintaining community status or achieving political status in such a way as to further complicate the problems of ethnic identity and relationships. It is true that issues, elements, factors, and criteria of social structuring have probably perpetuated discrete ethnic inheritances into modern time in India to a greater degree than in most other parts of the oriental world and that political alignment today tends to perpetuate these historic patterns to considerable degree. To the extent that such factors are significant, India is having a hard time becoming the single cultural society that China has long been. In its own way Ceylon faces the same kind of problems in becoming a single society. Even more serious was the case for Pakistan, where disjunct locations, language, and cultural mores combined to place too heavy a stress on the single-state political structure. The small states of Nepal and Bhutan possess latent but undeveloped patterns of a similar sort that have not yet strongly come to the fore.

Throughout the oriental world there is great variation in ethnic background, only Korea and Japan possessing such ethnic conformalities as do not intrude upon the cultural problems of national identity. The ardent political nationalisms shown in southern and southeastern Asia tend to institutionalize particular cultural systems around ethnic constituencies. These issues become primary in such young political states as Burma and Malaysia, but the whole cultural shatter belt of mainland southeastern Asia is suffering cultural pains derived in part from historic ethnic diversity.

Population, Growth, and Excess

Had the hoary progenitor of the Chinese agrarian system, Shen Nung (the Divine Husbandman), speculatively projected the population potential of the farming system he supposedly concocted, it is doubtful that he would have dreamed of a possible 750,000,000 inhabitants living on the Chinese soil, and if Siva (the Creator and the Destroyer in Hindu religion) has planned ahead for 650,000,000 human beings on the Indian subcontinent, it would likely have been in terms of their impending doom. Surely such figures as these are proof of the inherent ability of our earth to stand up to tremendous and long continued abuse. There simply are too many people in the oriental world for all of them to live the good life at its proper level in the present century. This statement makes no inference for other societies, populations, or levels of living elsewhere and it has no relation to the eventually potential population of human beings that could inhabit our earth with a vastly improved and universally applied set of technologies, but it does have relation to the continuing technologies of primary production still in use by most of the peoples of the oriental world. In good part, despite all the changes of the last century, too many people still are using the conceptual principles and basic technologies developed during the late Neolithic when sedentary intensive gardening first began to be practiced and when scattered small village communities began the growth that would produce the vast rural peasantry existing throughout the oriental world today.

It is likely, as the Neolithic revolution in primary production came to maturity, that a few parts of the oriental world already were among the dominant population centers of the earth. The slow formulation of the Chinese agrarian system on the upper North China Plain and the equally slow formulation of the Indian agrarian system in the Indus Valley in northwestern India (now Pakistan) crystallized into two very productive agrarian systems, approximately 3000 B.C. in each case, and the late hatching of large broods of agrarian villagers began the processes of regional agrarian expansion that were to develop the two most easily productive large lowland zones in the oriental world (Fig. 11). The thousands of archeologic sites of villages of North China of the third millennium B.C. attest this early spread. Other regional centers of population growth were later in their staging of primary growth patterns, and they were smaller in extent and more complicated in socio-economic organization, but they did produce populations that have fed the modern growth structure. We still know too little of the really early evolutionary development of population distribution in the oriental world to lay this pattern out regionally.

It is clear, however, that such localized and regional centers as the fringes of the Inland Sea of southern Japan, the coastal lands of southern Korea, the Song Hoi Delta of North Vietnam, the upper Ganges Valley of North India, the Krishna River valley of peninsular India, northern Ceylon, and the north coast of Java were among the areas that began producing regional populations at a date just prior to and just after the start of the Christian Era (see Fig. 11). A few centuries later such regional centers as the upper Mekong River delta zone, the Annamese coast of central Vietnam, the dry zone of Burma, the Szechwan Basin of west China, and the Cauvery River valley of southern peninsular India came to this level of development. Still later, in the eleventh to fourteenth centuries, came the population advances of the central Yangtze Valley, the Tonle Sap Basin of Cambodia, the wet zone of southwestern Ceylon, and the lower Ganges Valley of India. In these cases it is likely that more effective socio-political organization was a significant factor on top the local development of agrarian expansion. And, lastly, came the modern developments associated with the nineteenth century, wherein the entry of European technology and stimulus to trade and the genesis of modern political structuring were also factors. Associated with these late developments came the population expansion of the Bengal Delta, the deltas of the Irrawaddy and the Choa Phraya, the island of Java, the central section of Luzon Island in the Philippines, the Yangtze Delta of eastern China, and the re-expansion of central Japan. The deltas of the great rivers, the Irrawaddy, the Chao Phraya, the Mekong, and the Yangtze presented peculiar local environments with too great handicaps for earlier cultures possessing only simple technologies for coping with seasonal flood volumes. It was only in the nineteenth century when large-scale drainage canal systems could be installed in order to drain off flood volumes that agrarian development could spread out into the delta lands. The Mekong Delta was the last of these to be processed and even now its settlement is still not complete. Although canals are old in the inner margins of the Yangtze Delta, the seaward margins came into settlement at a late date.

Thus, feeding the modern population growth of the oriental world has been a successional series of regional centerings of extraordinary population growths over the last four millennia that have sparked rapid expansion in particular areas. Some of the earliest expansions spawned the settlers for some of the later developments, as northern Chinese moving into Szechwan and the Yangtze Valley, or southern Japan providing the base for modern Japanese expansion. A casual reading of history suggests that there are great patterns of decline, such as the supposed anomaly of the Khmer Empire of Cambodia. At its height in the fourteenth century the Khmer Empire is reputed at four million in population, chiefly resident in the basin of the Tonle Sap. The structure and glory of empire certainly disappeared later, and undoubtedly the casualties of war reduced the population somewhat, but there were still close to three million Cambodians in the late nineteenth century forming a quiet and rural agrarian community. Thus it is evident that not all Cambodians disappeared with the demise of the political empire. The history of China is well documented as to periods of unrest, militancy, and population decline, and the fragmentary economic histories of India and southeastern Asia contain many suggestions to the same end, but it is also clear that none of these periodic political turbulences really cut back population totals in any sharp degree. The oriental world came into the modern era with very large population totals and with several cases of high regional densities. This means simply that there was a huge base for the modern expansion and growth of population in the last two centuries.

In terms of the suggestive notations of the previous chapter that there were numerous regional environments that formed appropriate homelands in which culture groups could settle down and develop particular living systems, the population history of the oriental world suggests that there were many productive regional centers. Every modern regional political state is based on one of these regional entities. Every one of the environmental units has matured a regional variety of life and culture, and today each presents a nuclear core around which there has developed a sizable population that now is expanding outward from the core zone into the marginal lands on the perimeters of the region. The one modern political state, in terms of political geographers' contemporary maps, that has not developed a specific culture system, a strong agrarian base, and an expanding population is Laos, but this is an area that, by the model suggested, does not meet the basic requirements of a good environmental region.

Not all parts of the oriental world comprised good regional environments, of course, and there still are relatively empty zones and physical

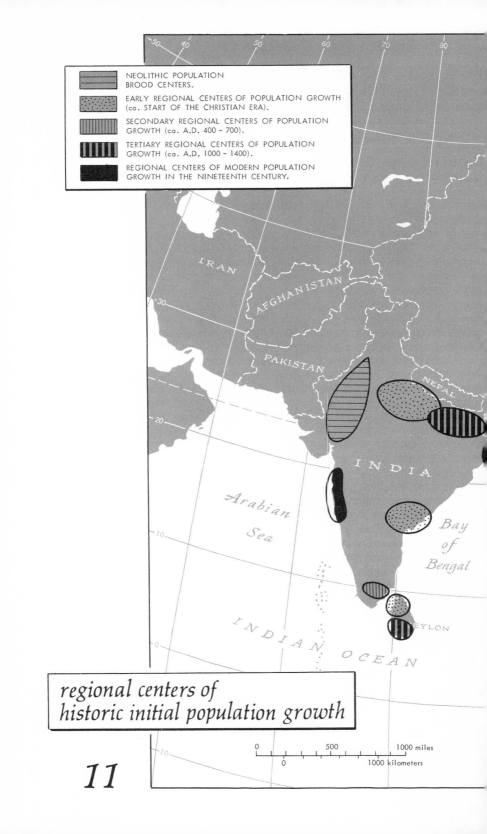

NEOLITHIC POPULATION
BROOD CENTERS.

EARLY REGIONAL CENTERS OF POPULATION GROWTH
(ca. START OF THE CHRISTIAN ERA).

SECONDARY REGIONAL CENTERS OF POPULATION
GROWTH (ca. A.D. 400 - 700).

TERTIARY REGIONAL CENTERS OF POPULATION
GROWTH (ca. A.D. 1000 - 1400).

REGIONAL CENTERS OF MODERN POPULATION
GROWTH IN THE NINETEENTH CENTURY.

IRAN

AFGHANISTAN

PAKISTAN

NEPAL

INDIA

Arabian Sea

Bay of Bengal

CEYLON

INDIAN OCEAN

*regional centers of
historic initial population growth*

0   500   1000 miles

0   1000 kilometers

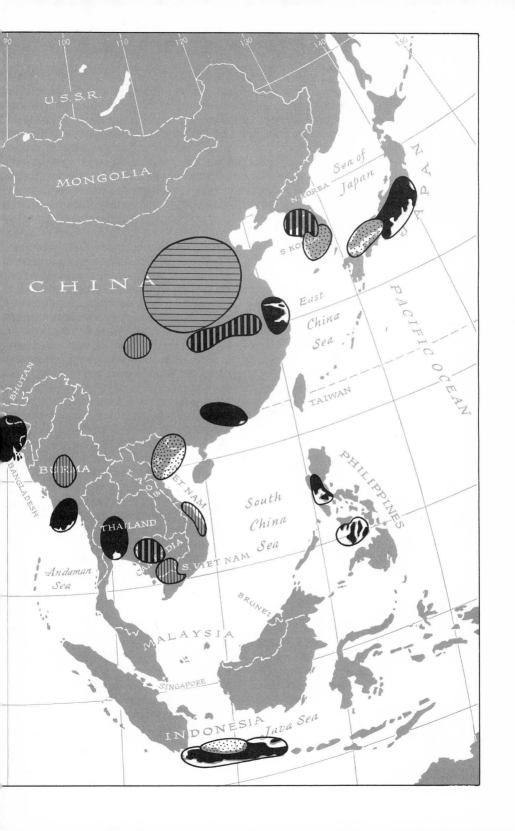

units that only now are coming under economic development and population settlement as the marginal lands of the realm. In each case, however, modern development is requiring large amounts of developmental capital to turn the areas into productive sectors. Notable among such regions is the island of Borneo, now divided between the states of Malaysia and Indonesia. The archeologic record suggests that Borneo had almost as much sampling by early man as did other parts of the island world, but in the critical period of the Neolithic no culture group picked Borneo as a good base for regional cultural development. Another island with a somewhat similar history is the large southern Philippine Island of Mindanao. The southern end of the Malay Peninsula, comprising what now is West Malaysia, was a point of landfall and a supply base for many groups of travelers-traders before it came under regional development of a significant sort. In the northern sector of the oriental world Manchuria represents a region with strong climatic contrasts and a summer short enough that no culture group in Neolithic times had the agrarian technology to master problems of development. Politico-military prohibitions were operative between the early centuries of the Christian Era and the late nineteenth century, when the matured Chinese agrarian system might have mastered the seasonal problems, so that it was only with the weakening of the Manchu restrictions on settlement that Manchuria came under development. Similarly, northern Honshu and Hokkaido presented not only physical problems but climatic ones as well to Japanese agrarian technology so that here too it was only in the nineteenth century that the Japanese northlands, with the aid of borrowed agrarian technologies from the Occident, came into development. The "Wisconsin dairy landscape" of northern Honshu and Hokkaido attests the widening of Japanese agrarian technology in the modern era.

The essential settlement system-agrarian system that everywhere was applied in the oriental world was that of intensive gardening, based on a large complement of human labor, cooperative working systems, and cooperative control of local landscapes. The village settlement system went hand in hand with aspects of social structure and agrarian technology. The basic systems resulted in the creation of small "farms" situated in close-order patterns around village bases. The pattern repeated across the landscape and the pattern expanded over the regional landscape as the population grew. Such a system built up high-population densities right from the start so that high per square mile population densities in the favored localities have been one of the primary characteristics of the oriental world, as the close-order spacing of archeologic sites for Neolithic North China clearly attests. In southern and southeastern Asia the archeologic record is thin and does not prove the case, but here it is well known that the bounteous restorative powers of the plant world quickly mask and then bury the human efforts at landscape control if those efforts falter and slacken for but a little while.

When favored localities reached what regional occupance considered a density pattern that enabled full control over the regional landscape, the normal historic process involved movement toward the margins of the region or in the direction in which the favored landscape extended in order to hold local densities at the proper levels. When regional landscapes became fully settled, further population increase of necessity migrated to more distant locations, finding other regional landscapes amenable of the standard treatment. Through centuries of this kind of expansion the northern Chinese settled Szechwan and the Yangtze Valley, eventually pushing into South China, and in this century settling Manchuria. Such southern resettlement programs placed pressures on the "barbarian" peoples occupying the respective regions, provoking the streams of migration into the southeastern mainland during the historic period. Somewhat similar patterns were operative in the Indian subcontinent, though the recurrent militant invasion by Islamic peoples somewhat masks the innate native patterns of expansion. The historic northward push of the Japanese through Honshu Island into Hokkaido represents a variant of the same pattern. In the modern period this is the procedure by which Luzon Island in the Philippines has filled to a very high density and resettlement in Mindanao has been brought about. It is the same pattern by which Vietnamese have progressively spread down the Annamese coastal plain and in the last century have been settling the Mekong Delta and moving in upon the Cambodians. Everywhere the same small-farm, close-order occupance system has again and again been reproduced.

By the beginning of the nineteenth century the good lowlands of China were filled to the old system's capacity, with only marginal country remaining open, Manchuria still not being available. Since population growth continued, there were two results from this kind of situation: (1) There began the concerted push into the hill and mountain country dividing China into lowland blocks, although there agrarian development often failed to achieve very high efficiency or adequate productivity, achieving instead the same kinds of densities on the restricted amounts of land that was arable. (2) The refusal of many villagers to leave the good lowlands began the process of piling up landless individuals and to divide the available land among more and more cultivators. Both actions contributed to the lowering of the level of living and the overloading of the agricultural landscapes. By about 1875 China began for the first time to import food supplies. By about 1930 the Chinese agrarian system had reached the end of the line at which increasing numbers of human laborers no longer could produce enough food and salable products to warrant their labor. Some kind of revolutionary change in the system was ripe for initiation, for none of the agricultural improvements introduced between 1900 and 1930 had been more than fractional palliatives.

In a similar fashion India was also close to the end of the line with its traditional agrarian system by the 1940's, although the passive resignment of Hindu India bore the stresses differently than did China. Accurate data on Indian land use are so scant that it is uncertain that the above date is correct, and recent shifts in land-use policies produce variable statistics concerning forests, croplands, and culturable wastes, but it does appear that the date is a good figure. The "green revolution" may have given both India and Pakistan a little time in which to mature industrialization and in which to make other adjustments, perhaps just barely to escape the kind of drastic change that came to China.

Elsewhere variable sets of conditions have obtained. Pakistan is in a position closely analagous to that of India. The new state of Bangladesh has only marginal lands remaining unoccupied and these are chiefly in the lower delta country where costs will be high and the hurricane hazard (tropical cyclone in Indian English) high, adding to the cost problem. West Pakistan has considerable arable land remaining open, but its arid climatic factors demand irrigation and future developments in this direction will be costly. It would appear that, except for northernmost Honshu and Hokkaido, the Japanese agrarian landscape reached its practical maximum extent by about the 1870's, with trade-offs balancing new lands brought under cultivation against land going into nonagricultural uses. The expansion of northern agricultural landscapes has slowed down recently so that the agricultural landscape has about reached its maturity. The Japanese program of industrialization has, of course, been the salvation of Japanese economy, for it not only has taken people off the land but it has also provided the increases in productivity that have enabled Japan to remain close to balanced food consumption-food production. Recent Japanese population policy has also acted to control population growth in a manner operative in no other oriental society to date. The Korean agricultural landscape appeared to reach its general maturity during the early 1940's, the Japanese forcing the last possible significant increases in total cultivable land.

North Vietnam reached the maturity of its agricultural landscape during the 1920's, but South Vietnam still has some reserve land available in the Mekong Delta country. Taiwan, in the late 1960's, was very close to its agricultural maturity in landscape terms, although some marginal lands are still being developed. Indonesia stands in the peculiar position of having lots of reserve land of better than marginal quality in the Outer Islands, but Java-Madura have no reserve lands remaining and Sumatra is gradually filling up. Ceylon has some fair area of land that could have been developed in the traditional system centuries ago, but under modern government controls and developmental systems it has only marginal lands remaining that will be costly to develop for agrarian occupance.

The other political states of oriental Asia all have short-term respites before their agricultural landscapes reach maturity. The Philippines, Cambodia, Thailand, Burma, and Malaysia have reserves of land that could be occupied under traditional or modernized technology for perhaps two more decades, but after that the costs of agricultural expansion will rise variably in each country. Already in each country the agrarian problem is coming to the fore, for each has local regions in which density patterns are excessive, and in each there is considerable migration taking place between such areas and the outer margins of the zones of worthwhile occupance. In each there are variable programs under government control that operate with minimal efficiency, and there are stresses in the agrarian circumstance that may provoke problems in every country.

Except for Japan every country in the Orient still faces rates of population growth that pertain to traditional systems of agrarian expansion. Since these rates range from 2.5% to around 4.0% the problem is rapidly becoming a critical one throughout the whole of the Orient. Much has been made recently of the "green revolution" as providing a whole new future to agricultural expansion, economic prosperity, and agrarian crises. If all goes well for all countries, the new lease on life for the agrarian economy does indeed augur that prospect, but it raises other problems. If total self-sufficiency in food production were to come everywhere in the Orient by 1973, what would happen to international trade patterns by which several oriental countries have depended on their crop exports to deficit regions for their sources of foreign exchange and purchases abroad? What would happen to the rates of population increase under short-term sufficiency in food supplies? What would happen to general international trade patterns? And what would happen if something suddenly were to go astray with the "green revolution"?

There is great hazard in attempting to quantify any of the above qualitative generalizations about populations during the period since the Neolithic, but some guesses are in order to put the matter of regional densities into perspective. Early Neolithic inhabitants of North China apparently used shifting cultivation as an agricultural system, for many sites show discontinuous but repetitive occupance. But the late Neolithic sites in the Chinese culture hearth region are those of sedentary occupance and permit some guessing. Small to large villages were thickly scattered in parts of the North China Plain, suggesting fairly full-scale land use in the regional sense. Undoubtedly not the whole of the arable surface was then in cropland, and the efficiency of the productive system cannot have been of a high order, but a population of 100 people per square mile may not be too far off the case in those culture hearth good lowlands that were easily utilized. The modern gross population densities of the North China Plain are on the order of 600–800 per square mile. If these figures are put into population per square mile of cultivated land, the Neolithic figure could be something on the order of 200–300, whereas in the modern era the same figure in the same area is on the order of 1,100–1,400. The relative efficiency of the agricultural system has increased greatly in terms of yield per acre of cultivated land, and there certainly is a higher share of the total arable land under crop today than was true in the Neolithic. But this modern density accents the nature of the problem inherent in the permanent dependence on an intensive gardening system. The culture hearth has spilled out generations of people who have populated the whole of China to the end that agricultural densities for all of China Proper today are somewhat alike. Whereas Neolithic surpluses could spin off into empty lands, there are no good empty lands in China Proper today.

The Song Hoi delta region of North Vietnam came into well-settled occupance before the start of the Christian Era. It has spun off the steady streams of southward moving Vietnamese who have occupied the Annamese Coastal Plain in the same intensive manner over the centuries, and the agricultural densities in the old Vietnamese hearth in the Song Hoi Delta are still among the highest in the world. In broad terms, this same pattern of piling up rural agricultural densities on the good lands has taken place everywhere in the Orient today. In such "new" areas as the delta of the Irrawaddy the traditional patterns have been reproduced, and the current program of settling Mindanao, in the Philippines, is also reproducing the same high-density small farmscape pattern found in Luzon, to the end that the earth has been pushed toward its maximum yield per acre for the production of food, textile, and exports products. The term "maximum," of course, is purely relative, for Vietnamese farmers get far less out of the land than do Japanese farmers, and Filipinos have never become as efficient as Chinese in achieving high productivity.

Another factor has been of increasing significance in the rural areas of dense population in the last few centuries. The advent of the European brought a totally new element into the handling of agricultural products in that increasing volumes of particular products were siphoned off into the growing pattern of international trade. And then, as the European industrial system matured, there began the European export of manufactured goods, the oriental world forming one segment of a world-wide market. As this continued, the regional import of manufactures began the undercutting of the regional systems of handicraft manufacturing that had always been part of the regional economic systems of the oriented world. During the nineteenth century regional handicraft manufacturing seriously declined everywhere throughout the oriental world, except in Japan and Korea, these regions remaining closed to the European. What happened, then, was that as the rural areas of the oriental world began to reach the limits of their agricultural expansion, those rural populations lost much of the rural handicraft market that had served as an economic complement in their regional economies. This, at a time when there were fewer possibilities of agricultural expansion, forced large numbers of rural agricultural peoples back into greater dependence on their agriculture, with population still growing steadily. The further fractionating of agricultural holdings among larger numbers of rural inhabitants has meant a steadily decreasing level of living for over a century.

One can only return to the generalizations that there are too many people in the oriental world today, that its traditional systems of agrarian living have brought the peoples of every country to the point of needing drastic change in the whole cultural system, and that industrialization and the "green revolution" may offer a little time during which systemic change may take place (Fig. 12). The drastic systemic change must include eventual population control systems for every country at least as efficient as those that have become operative in Japan in the period since World War II. Unless these patterns of change can be brought about within this century, the next century can only spell trouble for all portions of the oriental world.

It has been popular in some quarters to blame the Occident and its exploitive politico-economic programs for the whole pattern of declining levels of living in the oriental world. This opinion sometimes reaches the conclusion that only the socio-political constructs of the Communist World offer any solution. This is a form of beating a dead horse, sometimes becoming a species of political self-flagellation. Inherently, however, the results are the product of the too-long extended perpetuation of a culture system that worked well during the Neolithic and the early historic centuries, but a system that would have run its limits in time whether the West had ever come East or not. There is no significant evidence to the effect that any of the specific oriental culture systems made any effort to alter components of its basic system before the European came, and no such efforts were initiated after the European came, except for the case of Japan. There were no cultural currents moving toward primary alteration of any regional system, from inside that system, even after the European came, and had not Europeans forced Japan to examine her position, Japan would have not have moved toward alteration of the basic system when she did. Had the West never come East, it might well have been the course of events that reaching the end of the line would have been postponed for variable intervals of time, according to regional conditions. The conclusion is inescapable, however, that the basically agrarian orientation of the oriental world was so effective in producing enlarging populations that the system would eventually have created its own problem of too many people and no more empty lands.

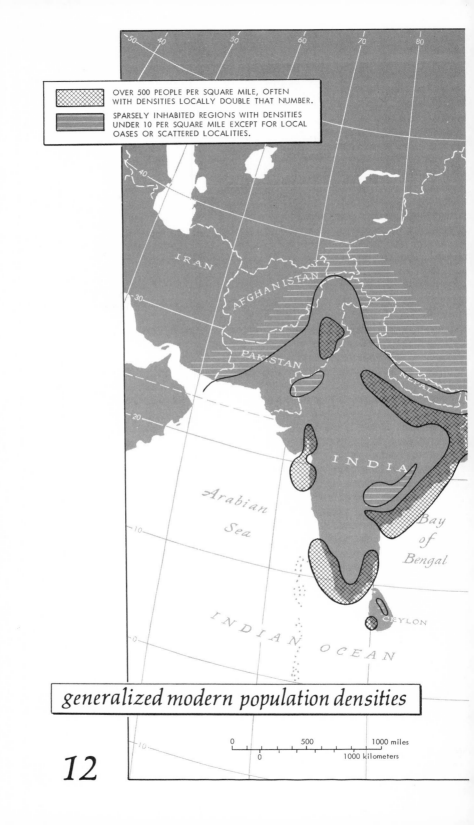

OVER 500 PEOPLE PER SQUARE MILE, OFTEN
WITH DENSITIES LOCALLY DOUBLE THAT NUMBER.

SPARSELY INHABITED REGIONS WITH DENSITIES
UNDER 10 PER SQUARE MILE EXCEPT FOR LOCAL
OASES OR SCATTERED LOCALITIES.

IRAN

AFGHANISTAN

PAKISTAN

NEPAL

INDIA

Arabian
Sea

Bay
of
Bengal

INDIAN OCEAN

CEYLON

generalized modern population densities

0   500   1000 miles

0   1000 kilometers

12

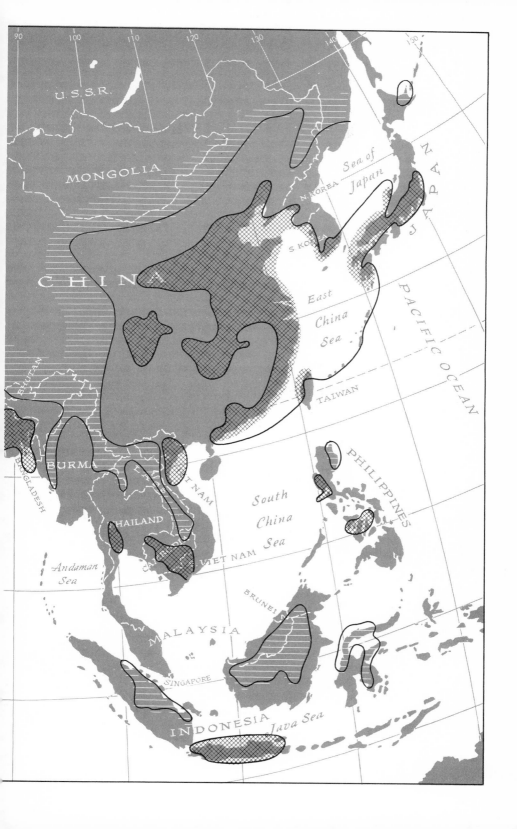

CHAPTER 4 *how peoples live: agricultural economies and living systems*

In the past the oriental world was primarily an agrarian world with a rather close contact with nature in the wild. Inferences to this end appeared in earlier chapters, and the burden of this chapter is to spell out the several systems in their basic patterns, to relate those systems to the regional zones of the oriental world, and to distinguish the newer trends in material economies. The modern oriental world is going through aspects of withdrawal from that natural wild world, of course, as industrialization takes hold and as men remold their lives in the fashion of urbanites elsewhere. One element in the withdrawal, however, has to do with the more complete making over of wild landscapes into cultural landscapes in which there are restrictions on the continuance of the wild and the setting up of more culturally controlled conditions. These developments have not taken place through the freely willful action of all societal groups within the ethnic spectrum, for there are many groups that have tried to cling to the more elemental economies even into modern time. However, in every major regional environment there have been ethnic groups that have forced the pace, pushed against the wild frontier, and elaborated their own systemic cultural landscapes and living systems, in effect restricting the territory still open to the pursuit of the simpler economies. Not in any sense of setting up stages of cultural-economic development, but in the sense of enumerating descriptive typologies this chapter briefly deals with the several kinds of living systems extant in the oriental world of the twentieth century.

Remnants as Groups and Systems

Three centuries ago one could have asserted flatly that in every major region of the oriental world except the Tibetan highland there were living societies that followed the practices of residential mobility, employed hunting and collecting as material economies, and used relatively simple communal social structures suggestive of Paleolithic levels of culture. Even in southernmost China, near the Vietnam border, was this true, as it was on Hainan Island and on Taiwan. Even three centuries ago, of course, these hunting and collecting societies already were distinctly minority groups undergoing decline, but they were still widely distributed and self-contained, operative societies. Originally living in the richest biotic realm of the earth these simple cultures early had tremendously wide-ranging possibilities as to daily food sources, freedoms of territorial range, and minimum controls by environmental conditions that required high specialization in any one direction. These groups lived both on land and on the coastal seas. None was truly nomadic, since each ethnic component operated within a particular resource range on a known annual sequence of mobility patterns, but it is likely that several groups were gradually withdrawing away from the frontiers of expanding societies. Along some coastal fringes some groups were ambivalent in terms of primary concern, seasonally dealing with aquatic resources or with land-based resources. Such groups were scattered from the western Himalayan foothills to eastern New Guinea and northward into Hokkaido, as land-based groups, and from Tenasserim to Celebes and the Sulu Sea as sea gypsies.

Within the last three centuries many of the former self-sustaining minority groups have come upon hard times, have found their last resource ranges being appropriated for other uses by other societies, and have either died out or have become submerged into the ethnic streams of those societies that have displaced them. The true hunting-collecting Veddas of Ceylon and South India are gone now, and the Ainu of northern Honshu and Hokkaido are reduced to a nonsustaining fractional society dependent on Japanese tolerance and largesse. The Negritoes of the Philippines no longer have ample territorial ranges but are forced to live as hangers-on around the fringes of mutilated or agricultural landscapes, able only to eke out a partial living from the remnants of the wild ranges. In India a few groups still attempt their traditional systems but the going is hard and will not be for long. In Bangladesh, Burma, Thailland, Malaysia, Cambodia, and Vietnam there remain fragmentary, scattered, and self-isolating small groups struggling to maintain their old systems of culture, living close to a vanishing nature, refugees from the open world they formerly knew, remnants that will soon vanish. In western Indonesia the last of the minority groups is disappearing, but there are a few groups operating autonomously in some of the less fully developed islands in eastern Indonesia, such as Celebes, Portuguese Timor, and Indonesian New Guinea. Only in interior Borneo and in interior New Guinea are there operating conditions at all conducive to the continuance of the old life, but even here there are militant neighbors pressing in upon the resource ranges and the debilitating conditions increase through time to prejudice future continuance.

Within the folds of the agricultural world in the broad sense are the ethnic groups that practice shifting cultivation as an integral system, seeking still to maintain their traditional culture systems that partake both of the world of cultivated landscapes and the world of wild nature (see Fig. 8). To these peoples shifting cultivation is a way of life, and settlement systems, social structures, governance, animism, a world view, and economic activities are integrated into a holistic system of life. Shifting cultivation as an agricultural technology, in these cases, is not a product of tropical environmental influences, as still stated in some elementary geography texts, but it is a technology articulated as one aspect of a Neolithic living system that in its time was the most progressive system known, and an advance upon the simpler Paleolithic systems. It must be interjected here that shifting cultivation, as a specific technological system of crop production, can be used by anyone right up to the culture level of the modern industrial world. Such technological crop systems, however, are partial systems only, using the cropping technology as the best means to a given end, whereas the other aspects of culture systems belong to diverse and complex patterns. A bulldozer can be used to clear a field in which to grow a crop for cash sale to an urban market, but the operator of the bulldozer is a member of an urban culture system a long culture distance removed from the culture system of the integral shifting cultivator.

Integral shifting-cultivator societies once made up the populations of much of the oriental world, just as they once made up the larger part of the population of the European peninsulas. Shifting-cultivator societies composed the advancing sectors of the ancient world, as opposed to the lagging cultures of the hunters-collectors. These were the peoples, working with both plants and animals in material economy, that we presume to be those who also worked with new aspects of social structuring, elements of governance of groups, elements of nature worship shaped into animistic codes, and those features of domestic life that go with new systems. In short these are the folk who summed up new living systems in what we now term culture hearths. These are the folk who also first began to grow in numbers at compound rate to provide the spinoff groups that were the basic migrants of the ancient world, the underpinnings of ethnic regionalisms that gave rise to the populations of the modern world.

Integral shifting cultivators practice essentially long-range land rotation systems, using particular methods in achieving plantable garden patches that accord ecologically to biotic and climatic environments. Shifting cultivators always utilize collecting, however, as a practical and normal complementary economic function, or as a famine-period substitution during those years in which the climatic sequences were abnormal. Calendric cycles vary with zonal climatic controls, material operational sequences relate to specific environmental regionalism and to particular cropping combinations followed, social organizations and structures derive from inherited tradition based upon inherent world views, and settlement systems are those preferred as practical in terms of spatially ordered patterns of land occupance. When shifting cultivators are free to arrange these matters by choice, their occupance of particular regions is ecologically sound and in biotic balance, with little destructive impact upon the environment. Regional landscapes then show local variations in patterns of forest maturity, regeneration stages, and siting of currently operative cropped sites. Population patterns reflect levels of technological complexity in holistic culture systems in that very simple and young systems normally achieve only low density populations, whereas mature systems that have achieved complex technologies efficient in productivity may reach quite high population densities. Such population patterns may range from five people per square mile to about five hundred per square mile. Eastern Mindanao showed the lighter density pattern as late as 1930, whereas highland eastern New Guinea now clearly demonstrates the possible higher density range.

From the richest of the world's flora there gradually came a large number of plant domestications. Within the oriental world, according to manner of ordering, there are several domestication regions, each with a fairly large range of plants (see Fig. 4). Such root crops as the taros and yams appear to be extremely old, complemented by other vegetatively reproduced roots, and rhizomes, including such fruits as the banana. Slowly the seed-planted crops have replaced the vegetative crops, but it is unclear what role the shifting cultivator had in bringing these into domestication in the early periods. Rice, the modern mainstay of the oriental agricultural economy, appears to have been a relatively late domestication and it may have been post-Neolithic in the full sense. Millet appears to be older than rice in most portions of the oriental world, and it may have been properly a Neolithic domesticate by shifting cultivators.

Within the last millennium, particularly, shifting cultivators throughout the oriental world, and the simpler hunting-collecting cultures too, have been under increasing pressure from the advanced societies who create permanent cultural landscapes. This pressure has meant territorial restriction, conquest, settlement by infiltration, operational restriction by laws, and political restriction by dominant overlords. Such pressures have come from native oriental states and from European colonial overlords. New concepts of land control instituting private ownership by individuals and government preserves by colonial overlords placed intolerable spatial restrictions on the politically weak shifting-cultivator societies. Their long-range rotational systems became ecologically unbalanced, resulting in soil erosion, deterioration of vegetative cover and animal populations, and dissolution of social organizations. In areas most exposed to the various systems of control shifting-cultivator societies broke down, their territories were taken over by permanent-field occupants, and the permanent cultivated landscapes expanded. Sometimes migration into less controlled mountain country enabled the continuance of the shifting-cultivator society, but often its fractionated members became submerged by the increasing populations of the expanding society taking over the territory.

Today shifting cultivation is basically a remnantal agricultural economy practiced in the hill and mountain country throughout the southern oriental world, with a few small remnants still operational in the partial-system sense in the higher hill country of central and western China, northern Korea, and in the highlands of Japan (see Fig. 8). From the Philippines southward shifting cultivation still is practiced among those simple culture groups that have resisted integration into the cultural systems of the national political states controlling territory. As a remnantal system it remains operative because it is the only practical system of using much of the rough country for agricultural production; therefore, its retention by the simpler ethnic groups has sound practicality. There are no open and empty lowlands into which such groups could be resettled. Political administration of the national states of the southern Orient cannot yet reach into all the rough highlands in such effective terms as to prohibit shifting cultivation or to replace it by other forms of practical economy.

Throughout the southern oriental world perhaps two hundred and fifty million acres of land are utilized sequentially in shifting cultivation, with an annual clearance for cropping of perhaps forty million of those acres. Almost fifty million people are involved in shifting cultivation, although not all of these now are full-scale integral shifting cultivators. A share of the annual clearance is by the frontier permanent settler who is in the process of establishing a permanent-field farm. Unable to achieve total clearance of his intended farm in a single year, he proceeds sequentially over a period of years, using an obvious technology, but never permitting the long-range regeneration in wild growth of previously cleared plots. The share of clearance-cropping by integral shifting cultivators is slowly declining as the permanent-field cultivator edges steadily deeper into the old domain of the integral shifting cultivator.

Almost all shifting cultivators are members of ethnic minorities living apart from primary populations and having their own socio-political structures and controls. Almost all are animistic in religion, their world views, religious beliefs, ritual practices, and calendric intervals tied closely to the operational aspects of their material economy. Almost all are villagers who live in straggling to compact settlements ranging from a dozen to a thousand houses. Few shifting-cultivator villages possess the amenities of civilized settlements, i.e., stores, markets, fairgrounds, formal religious structures, community centers, medical clinics, and other such advanced institutional features. Houses are both homes and handicraft production centers for clothing and tools. Hardly anyone has access to transport facilities beyond the human porter (and the occasional pack animal available in the northern mainland sector of southeastern Asia). Daily life and social intercourse revolve around the ritualized work schedules relating to clearing, cropping, and harvesting. Slack-season hunting expeditions, trading ventures, and militant protective operations provide breaks in annual routines.

Shifting cultivation and the integral life that goes with it are remnant patterns left over from the Neolithic. These patterns are gradually receding in spatial terms, declining in numerical terms, and suffering dissipation in holistic cultural terms as the permanent-field landscape continues to encroach and as the outside populations find ways of access into the more remote hinterlands with the "civilizing" processes, goods, and restrictive controls. Such living systems, once advanced, now are lagging elements in the life and economy of the oriental world.

The Peasant Gardeners

Just where in the Old World there began the basic elements of sedentary village dwelling and permanent-field cropping practices is neither possible to state nor critical to the discussion of regional variants. The basic elements show up both in North China and North India before the historical record has clarified the beginnings of advanced political structures. Whether or not there were more regional sources within the oriental world is also hard to state clearly, and it is not critical. The two basic systems appear to have spread their influences throughout the oriental world in variable degree. Both systems initially were simple hoe cultures in which human labor was applied to small plots of ground by the use of simple tools. Both were the essential technology which, combined with other cultural patterns, gave rise to the peasant agricultural systems that have been the mainstay of the oriental world's economy for well over two thousand years.

In North China this basic hoe culture began around small village societies having tightly knit social structures that permitted the growth of a close-order cultivated landscape in which cooperative labor sharing was a regular matter. Within this Chinese social structure large families providing a labor force produced a growing system that grew better technologically and expanded spatially. The Chinese system made use of the pig, the dog, the chicken, the duck, and possibly the pheasant as integral elements of their gardening system, the animals not only providing food but fertilizers. It is not clear just when the use of human wastes as fertilizers came into usage, but gradually the Chinese gardener came to use all the forms of organic fertilizers that were available, not only maintaining soil productivity but also improving the quality of soils in the immediate hinterland around villages. Crop patterns centered on wheat and millet as staples, a variety of vegetables and fruits domesticated within North China, and a steadily increased set of crop plants periodically added to from outside the hearth region. A few centuries prior to the start of the Christian Era the plow tools came into China and entered into a complementary position in agriculture, being used by those who could afford them and possessed the right kinds of lands. The use of large domestic animals in the food economy became regularized, as did their use in local transport, but the use of milk products never became accepted in China. However, the basic aspects of Chinese agriculture did not change much with these new elements but remained essentially a small-plot intensive gardening procedure that gave large returns from productive soils located close around the sedentary villages. Animal pasturage never became a significant element in land use. As Chinese settlement spread out from the hearth region, the basic system was carried to new regions and ecologically fitted to the landscape and climatic cycle.

Above the villages stood the regionally spaced cities that already had become part of the Chinese cultural structure, with varying patterns of political administration that gradually settled into the *hsien,* or county, system based on an administrative city, several counties being grouped into a political region. Private land ownership systems had also come into vogue just prior to the start of the Christian Era, and with this addition the basic Chinese system came to maturity. Land became the primary economic good, the large family with numerous sons was the basic unit, an intensive cropping system provided surplus food supplies that supported the cities from whence came some of the finer consumer products that could not be produced by rural handicrafts. With an urban scholar bureaucracy at the top of the social scale, the rural peasant farmer stood next in status, and the Chinese peasant economy achieved stability.

As the centuries passed and the Chinese cultural state expanded, peasant economy both faced new regional environments and added to its basic crop complement. South China's watery lowlands developed an economy primarily based on rice as a wet-field crop, but the intensive gardening system prevailed (see Fig. 4). In every century after about A.D. 200 some significant new crop plant come into China to fit into some regional economy in ecological terms. And as Chinese influences spread beyond China the basic elements of intensive gardening spread also, to Korea, Japan, and Vietnam in the earlier centuries, and those same elements also went with the Chinese who later became resident in the Philippines, Thailand, Malaysia, and Indonesia.

In early northwest India lies another regional center of a peasant agricultural system that began essentially as an intensive gardening system. Here also there evolved a close-order village system around which tightly knit social structures and cooperative labor patterns made for a firmly established cultivated landscape. The village communities of India probably were more interlocking in social organization that those of China, since spinoff groups establishing secondary and tertiary villages maintained their lineage alignments with the home village to a greater extent. More is made of Indian village democracy than for China, but political superstructures developed above the Indian village, and the Indian concept of kingship was that of a more powerful ruler than in China. The elaboration of religious institutions achieved far more complications on the Indian subcontinent than anywhere else in the oriental world, eventually dividing the populace into highly segregated classes via the most complex of the earth's systems of social stratification. Unlike China, in India the agrarian strata became positioned toward the bottom of the structure.

The Indian system gradually evolved along somewhat different lines from the Chinese system. The hazards implicit in the Indian monsoonal climatic regime early made the development of local water supplies and irrigation into traditional elements. The Indo-Aryan invaders of early India were cattle users whose intrinsic crop-growing technologies were comparatively undeveloped, so that animals became integrated into the early system more fully than in China, although formay animal pasturage has not been a part of normal land use. The use of milk products, the use of the plow tools and draft animals, and the use of animal transport were more highly developed than in China. There evolved a taboo on killing the cow, a taboo that expanded its application into a prohibition on killing any animal, bringing about the growth of a vegetarian food economy in a culture that used domestic animals extensively. The use of the plow tools and draft animals seems fully characteristic of Indian agriculture, yet the evolving social stratification accumulated a large agrarian population too poor to own such equipment, so that a very large share of energy put into crop growing involves human labor, and the Indian system as a whole never clearly evolved beyond the levels of a gardening system. Millets and wheat were basic in the northwest at the start and, as in China, rice became a primary crop in the humid lowlands, but Indian grains achieved a wider range of variety in early India than in China, and the seasonal planting-harvesting regimes became more intricate than in the mono-seasoned North China (see Fig. 4).

The use made of animals in the Indian case is different from that of China. Although the pig was utilized in earliest India, a taboo did evolve against it and, as the evolution of the general taboo on killing animals evolved, the Indian gardener made little use of the pig, the dog, the chicken, and the duck, so basic to Chinese intensive gardening. The Indian system never included the consistent and careful use of fertilizers and other soil-building procedures. In some regions of the subcontinent the use of animal manures on the land slowly became normal practice, but in many regions the animal manures have long been the primary source of domestic fuel. The Indian never became the careful and fully efficient gardener that characterized the Chinese, and the per acre yields for the subcontinent have always been lower than those for China. Private land ownership did not apparently become regularized on the subcontinent until at least the late fourth century A.D., although the religious institutions had long been awarded control over productive cultivated lands.

Indian political, religious, and social complications seem to have inflicted more problems on the development of an agrarian peasantry and its agricultural systems than is true for China, and the Indian rural peasantry achieved a lower position in society than in China, but the end result was the development of an agrarian peasantry that practiced agricultural systems having some vertical variation. At the upper level was a generalized system akin to a plow culture utilizing dairying but not meat products. At the lower level the system remained an intensive gardening system that was not extremely efficient and that was largely vegetarian out of necessity but not so fully restricted by dietary taboos as were the upper levels. That India never eliminated the "non-Indian" groups, in the way in which the Chinese pressured most "non-Chinese" into acceptance or emigration, the Indian picture remains clouded by regional variances that tend to confuse the generalization about the subcontinent. The Indian patterns were spread outside of India into Ceylon, southern Burma, Thailand, Cambodia, and western Indonesia in the early period, and their influences have been evident throughout the whole of southeastern Asia.

Beyond the two large mainland zones of the Indian subcontinent and China variant versions of sedentary intensive gardening evolved, variably in time and bearing some relationship to one of the earlier models. Each became a peasant agrarian system based on the closely knit village clustering pattern, developing a local landscape that gradually expanded against the wild landscape or the landscapes of the shifting-cultivator societies. Western Indonesia may have been the earliest of these to get started, centering on Java and a few local regions of Sumatra, taking after the Indian patterns in many respects. Korea and North Vietnam achieved their basic systems by the second century A.D., and Japan by the fifth century A.D., essentially after the Chinese model. Burma reached this level by about the ninth century and Cambodia by the tenth century at least, perhaps more Indian than Chinese. The Thai peoples had been operating essentially a Chinese system in southwest China before they began moving down into their modern homeland. The Spanish began converting the mobile shifting-cultivator and sea-using Filipinos to a variant of the system in the early seventeenth century, and West Malaysia perhaps reached an equivalent system by the end of the seventeenth century. The pattern elaborated in the Philippines owes its landscape morphology to the Spanish New World rather than to China or India and owes its social structuring in part to Christendom, but many aspects of native culture persisted through the restructuring. The Malay case is less solidly the development of a full agrarian peasantry with a tightly structured pattern of regional development, but to the degree that the Malay states did develop their land-based territorial structures and economies the Malays fit into the same broad pictures. The nineteenth-century British concept of the Malay as a rural agrarian villager concerned with his rice fields and village gardens is that of an agrarian peasantry unwilling to alter its living system to fit British interests.

The classical occidental concept of the peasantry, of course, signified a medieval European rural agrarian society in some form of servitude to regional holders of political power and economic wealth, a rustic village society practicing a rude version of a regional culture, a conservative tradition-bound subculture dependent on urbanized consumers of local surpluses who also were originators of the more esoteric aspects of regional culture in mores and goods, a self-contained rural society born into its inherited status of being dependent yet self-perpetuating. The exact configurations of "peasantry" have been steadily changing since medieval times, and world-wide patterns of peasantry show many variations from the classic European model. There are some grounds for asserting that the state of peasantry has dissipated in modern times, but the position is here taken that the effective conditions of peasantry have merely been altered by changes in world culture since the tenth century, and that the rural agrarian sector of any heavily populated portion of the oriental world operates within the framework for which the term peasantry still is quite applicable. The contemporary peasant is subjected to different kinds of controls and pressures than formerly, and his degree of self-contained isolation in a rural countryside practicing a particular subculture is less stringent than it was a millennium ago, but the controls are no less effective in many respects.

It might be argued that the Communist takeover in North Korea,

China, and North Vietnam has liberated the agrarian rural resident from his former servitude, but the argument seems academic and empty. A rural Chinese villager today is more thoroughly controlled by outside political power than ever before, there remains the clear distinction between the rural agrarian and the urban political, the level of living in the commune village obviously has fewer attractions than urban life, and the controls over the elements of culture as dictated by national decision-makers have removed even the possibilities of local self-determination and self-containment. Similarly, it could be argued that a poor, rural village boy in Central Luzon, Indonesia, or India inherits his status today as fully as ever before. The Gandhian *khadi* (home manufacture) movement essentially perpetuated the peasant system in India, the varying self-help programs are attempts to alleviate the problems of the rural peasant, and the various government attempts at rural resettlement, seldom very efficient, are obvious in their recognition of problems that belong only to an overcrowded peasantry. Therefore, the discussion of oriental peasantry must come into the contemporary period.

As one examines the agricultural structure of the contemporary oriental world, one sees that the conclusion is inescapable that the predominant element in that structure is that of the peasant cultivator, resident in the majority of the 1,500,000 villages, working a small area of land (perhaps fragmented into several pieces) with very simple tools, using a large amount of human labor, having few capital resources for investment in productive improvement (in the Communist lands having only arbitrarily allocated work points as his annual return), burdened by taxation and disadvantageous obligations to landlord or moneylender from whom there is no real escape (or in Communist lands chancing the enforced "re-education" of the deviant or defiant), facing uncertain markets for his product (in Communist lands facing the centralized control over percentage of delivery of the yield), and beset by numerous kinds of restrictive regulation by government. These conditions are fully as limiting as were any of the forms of servitude in classical occidental situations.

In the oriental world today it is among the peasantry in the crowded lowlands that severe underemployment exists, since there are too many people and too little productive land (see Fig. 12). The alternative in the non-Communist countries is migration to the town and city, but in the Communist countries even that freedom customarily is being denied most of the time. It is here that one sees most clearly that the classical agrarian systems that evolved in the oriental world, by which intensive gardening culture achieved high productivity (as compared to older systems), have finally run aground by producing too many peasants. The desperate programs of industrialization that are being carried forward are an attempt to absorb this surplus production of peasants, but only in Japan has the program so far been successful.

Village life everywhere in the oriental world is still the rural life of the small community isolated in large degree in the agricultural countryside and concerned more with local affairs than with those of the national leadership groups. Village life has improved somewhat in the last hundred years in that contact with, and products of, the world at large no longer are totally impossible to attain. But life still is simple, the amenities are scant, and activity is circumscribed by the seasonal agricultural routine. For example, although India has brought wheeled transport and electric light to thousands of villages, electric light in 1971 still was not available in four-fifths of all villages. Although no obedient Chinese villager now faces starvation because of crop failure in his locality, rural housing has so far received little attention, the house with a single room for a family continues to predominate, and there are almost none of the amentities present. The Korean villager's chief concerns beyond looking after his fields are the marketing of his crops, the continuance of proper status relationships in his local community, and the proper selection of a wife for his marriageable son. A Balinese villager's primary current concern may be for the maintenance of his status in his local irrigation society in order to ensure water for his remaining wet-field rice plot after having sold one of his two plots fed by the society canal in order to repay his debt to the village treasury, that debt increased by the high bride-price required for his son's marriage. Although children may attend the village school quite regularly in most portions of the Orient today, the chief objectives in rural education remain those related to the land and its crops, the skills focussed around agricultural processes, the skills related to domestic crafts and daily chores, and the learning of the local community mores. Recreational activities of life chiefly are restricted to the simple patterns of traditional village rituals, ceremonials, and festivities, these taking up only a portion of the leisure hours during the year. Today the transistor radio is widespread in some countries, e.g., Japan, Taiwan, and the Philippines, and in some regions itinerant distributors and government agents occasionally take movies out into villages for exhibition under improvised conditions. Although many villages now have members absent from the village (through migration to town or city) and enjoy both the periodic visits from those migrant members and the occasional bringing home of "city goods," these neither effectively relieve the monotony of daily life nor provide the amenities that lift life above the rustic and rural. And although women in the villages today share some small fraction of the general emancipation of women throughout the oriental world, the daily routine still is arduous and endless because the equipment of the village home is minimal, traditional, and requires constant attention.

Within the Communist sector of the oriental world there have been many changes, of course, but these do not really alter the basic rural aspect. Here Communist policy and procedure have been to destroy the tight linkage of the village community, clan, family, and district political structure. Destruction has aimed both at structure of the peasant community and at content of life style, the better to bring the local community under control by the new national system. Many of the actions of Communist parties in North Korea, China, and North Vietnam, though seemingly irrational to the individualistic American as to motive, economic viability, and ultimate success, have had behind them specific rationale related to the self-subsistent independence of the rural peasant village. But for all the change in control of the land and in social and political mores, the rural populations of the three countries remain rural peasantry still, concerned with the evermore intensive cultivation of the land, since they cannot be employed usefully in large numbers in the towns and cities at this stage of industrialization. The peasantry remain the rural masses upon which so much of the burden rests in the rebuilding of nationalized Communists states, always urged to over-fulfill the annual quotas and constantly subjected to appropriate education within each state. In these lands life is full, arduous, and hazardous still, concerned with production by day, education by night, and the constant safe attunement of word and deed to the party line. Although the specific daily routines have been altered, the rites and mores replaced, and a modicum of security found for those obediently accepting the dictates by leadership, the rude life of the peasant villager still is dull and difficult as evidenced by the efforts of those "sent down" to return to the cities.

Only in Japan has the dissipation of the rural peasantry been achieved, for the majority of the population today resides in urban areas. The Japanese rural village population today involved only in the traditional life of the peasantry is very small indeed. Many of the nearly six hundred cities of Japan do retain suburban agricultural enclaves and fringes. The agricultural labor force has dramatically declined in recent decades, and a large share of the rural-resident agricultural families today have members participating in urban nonfarm occupational activities. The distribution of electricity, running water, radio, television, telephone service, the daily paper, and urban consumer goods now reaches all parts of Japan, so that almost every rural family may participate in most aspects of modern Japanese life. The transport systems of Japan now promote an intense mobility for the greater share of the population. Although many urban-resident living Japanese were rural-born, almost all maintain close connections with their home villages and towns, so that Japanese rural and urban living systems are becoming fairly well integrated today, to the end that the rural peasantry has evolved into a national citizenry. The agricultural system of Japan remains an intensive gardening culture, except in northern Honshu and Hokkaido where extensive occidental elements are found, but modern equipment and modern technologies have turned it into a small-scale industrial agriculture.

The landscapes created by sedentary peasant cultivators vary according to the zonal climatic controls, the nature of the regional cropping systems, and the variety of wild vegetation that remains tolerated. There is, however, a common denominator element in all such landscapes, the small-scale patterns and the mixed complexities that repeat themselves over and over. Comments were made in an earlier chapter on the kinds of landscapes that are to be seen in different sections of the oriental world (see Fig. 8). Rarely are holdings truly monocrop since each cultivator operates with as large a cropping combination as possible in his ecologic environment. Since much of the landscape has been terraced in some degree, the cultivated landscapes become patchwork mosaics in many regions, with repetitive themes repeated again and again in very slightly different precise combinations. That precise detail and the smallness of scale, within any region, overwhelms the traveller with a sense of sameness until one learns to watch for the minute variations that result from individual cultivator practices.

The Commercial Plantation Landscapes

One very distinct mark on portions of the oriental landscape today is that created by the plantation or estate agricultural system. A particular commercial economy has evolved around it, and there also are specific living systems related to the normal plantation. It is customary to attribute the plantation to the European political colonialism of the southern Orient, though the genetic elements have diverse origins. The term "plantation" earlier referred to a commercial planting of some crop plant, whereas the term "estate" referred more to land management and the handling of the commercial product. It is likely that Chinese initiated plantations in several parts of mainland southeast Asia and the island world, planting sugar and perhaps some of the spices, before the European entered the commercial export trade in agricultural commodities. For the European the plantation system originated in the early post-Columbian New World, and the system was brought into the Orient only after other methods of stimulating agricultural production failed to achieve their desired ends. Early European traders had difficulty in securing adequate volumes of export crop products in desired grades at comparable prices because the peasant village communities of the oriental world were not easily amenable to production of large volumes of surpluses in standardized grades. Several kinds of efforts at stimulating export production, such as the Dutch Culture System employed in Indonesia, preceded the establishment of the European plantation, and the modern plantation system dates only from the early nineteenth century in the southern Orient.

A plantation is essentially a large holding of land on which a single crop plant is grown, the labor being supplied by a work force resident on or near the plantation, the production normally going into commercial sale to a market located at a distance (Fig. 13). Owners of plantations seldom live on them, and managers are employed to run the operations, the labor force normally being made up of residents native to the region or by persons imported from some other region. There is no common definition for all countries of the minimal sizes of agricultural holdings that classify as plantations, the real distinction lying in how the operations are handled and who makes up the labor force. Holdings that are worked by owners normally are smaller than those worked by hired labor forces, and a common distinction in the literature classifies holdings under 100 acres as "smallholdings," with "estates" being larger than that figure, but this is an arbitrary distinction. In the modern period most European-owned estates are held by public corporations, but increasingly

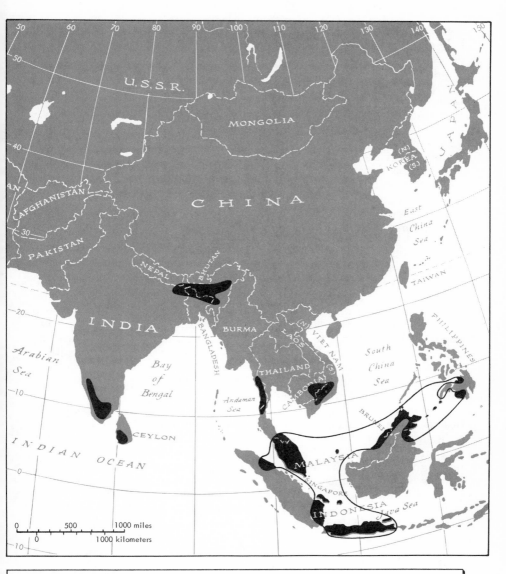

the locations of plantation holdings in agriculture

13

ownership of estates is passing to natives of oriental countries, as publicly held corporations, as private holdings operated by management agencies, or as private holdings operated by owners.

In its earlier oriental development the plantation utilized what the Europeans conceived as "vacant" lands located near an agricultural village community in order to utilize the labor force available in the village. In reality, almost all these lands were the reserve lands of shifting cultivators, vacant because they were undergoing regenerative growth under natural forest. Often such lands really "belonged" to the village community under the old native land systems operative in the several regions of the oriental world. European political controls introduced European concepts of land ownership, normally declaring all uncultivated lands to be "Crown Lands" under the control of the new political rulers. Such "vacant" lands were then eligible for issue either on outright ownership or long-term lease to Europeans wishing to establish plantations. Some variant of this system was applied all through the nineteenth century after the 1820's in India, Ceylon, Burma, Indonesia, and Vietnam. In the Philippines no plantations for commercial production had been established by the end of Spanish control. American land policy in the Philippines attempted to prevent the growth of the plantation system and did largely succeed in preventing large areas going into such developments, but it did not prevent the process entirely since legal subterfuges were occasionally employed to amass large holdings, and the maximum size category was large enough to permit effective commercial agricultural operations. American land policy also did not effectively break up more than a token share of the large holdings accumulated by Filipinos or the Roman Catholic Church during the Spanish era.

In India plantation development did find peasant village communities adequate to the labor requirements of the northern Indian tea plantations. In Ceylon, however, labor shortages developed and a large force of Tamils from southern India was imported to work the growing plantations, giving rise to the problem of ethnic communalism in the domestic politics of contemporary Ceylon. In Indonesia nearby village communities successfully provided labor forces in Java in the earlier period, but in modern times the Sumatran rubber plantations have had to import labor forces. In West Malaysia the Malays were early disinclined to work as laborers on British-owned plantations, leading to the hiring of immigrant Chinese and to the importation of Indian labor forces on short-term contract. Here, too, the plantation system has contributed to the ethnic pluralism of Malaysia since many of the Indians and many of the Chinese did not leave the country. In Vietnam-Cambodia almost all plantations were located in southern Vietnam and eastern Cambodia. The French recruited their plantation labor forces from the central Annamese coast and from Tonking, most of these laborers eventually leaving the plantations, after short periods, to become settlers in nearby areas, thus contributing to the southward drift of migration within the former French colonial holding of Indochina.

In the cases in which nearby peasant village communities supplied labor forces for the European plantations the two agricultural systems have operated side by side, the peasant system providing for itself and its surpluses being used by the increased population that also provided the labor force for the plantation. In that case a mixed landscape results, the one constituting the traditional complex and mixed mosaic of small holdings and the other the extensive monocrop landscape dominated by the physiognomic pattern of the particular crop plant being cultivated. The tea estates of northern India have been of this kind, and many of the remaining Indonesia sugar and tea estates of Java present this dual landscape.

In regions in which plantations are established on lands far from village settlements the landscape often is a more monotonous one, particularly in the regions in which rubber plantings are dominant. The green uniformity of rubber tree forests does break seasonally during the winter dry spell, when an extensive leaf drop occurs and the green tone turns dull and is varied by yellows and browns, but the uniformity remains monotonous. Labor forces often are housed right on the plantations themselves in village-like communities often termed "labor lines," for the houses are often built in uniform pattern along service roads. Here the complex mosaic of the peasant agricultural undertaking is absent, for the food supplies must normally be imported from more distant areas. Ceylon, West Malaysia, South Vietnam-Cambodia, and Sumatra show landscapes that often lack the duality present in the other case. Out of the development of this kind of plantation agriculture has come the requirement for large annual imports of food supplies to Ceylon, Malaysia, and Indonesia.

Coffee was the first of the plantation crops in the early nineteenth century, followed by tea and sugar. Various attempts were made at other crops but there were a number of failures. At the end of the nineteenth century the planting of rubber began in Ceylon and West Malaysia, and it is the rubber landscape that has become the dominant feature of the plantation system in southern India, Ceylon, Malaysia, Indonesia, and southern Vietnam-Cambodia. The Philippines is just now allowing the development of rubber production on leased plantations because the Philippine demand for rubber products has grown to the point that it proves a drain on foreign exchange. In the last two decades Borneo has been added to the plantation zone also, with both rubber and coconut as the products sought. Coffee no longer is a plantation product anywhere in the oriental world, but the African oil palm has been added to the landscape in West Malaysia and Indonesia.

At the present time rubber, oil palm, and coconut are the chief plantation products of Malaysia, and the rubber landscape is the dominant one. In Indonesia sugar cane, tea, coconut, and rubber are the dominant items. In Ceylon tea plantations dominate the upland landscape, rubber landscapes occupy the foothill zones, and coconut landscapes dominate the lower plains of south central-southwest Ceylon. Tea and rubber in relatively small-scale patterns appear in southern India, and in northern India the tea plantations stretch along the foothills of the Himalayas and into the Assam Valley. In the Philippines the coconut forests have been the dominating landscape element.

The plantation system has created problems in the southern Orient, despite its economic successes and the present importance of its yield to world trade. Because land that was not actually vacant in the full sense went into European control local populations were frequently deprived of their lands in outright terms, and this has created a long-term political sore point. Because plantations continued operations in areas in which peasant agricultural populations were reaching dangerous densities there has long been pressure on the land as a whole. This had taken a political direction in several regions before the granting of independence, as in Ceylon and Indonesia. Political pressures in the newly independent states have trended in the direction of confiscation of plantation lands in favor of allocation to peasant proprietors despite the obvious need to continue earning foreign exchange by maintaining the export of commercial products. It is likely that the future of the plantation system is limited in Vietnam-Cambodia, Ceylon, and Indonesia, although there may well be the continuance of selected plantations under strict controls. In Malaysia, both East and West, the plantation system is not in severe political straits and may well expand considerably. Long prevented in the Philippines, it may be that the plantation system will be expanded there.

The Smallholder and the Growth of Commercial Agriculture

In its traditional development the peasant village agricultural world of the Orient was primarily a regionally self-operating system. Sufficient surpluses of crop commodities and handicraft products always reached the towns and cities, and the civil bureaucracies of the political states, to support them and small volumes of particular products always moved in interregional exchange to maintain what amounted to a going system of international trade. As European and American traders began searching for products of interest to the rest of the world in the initiating of the modern patterns of large-volume international trade, those efforts gradually resulted in stimulating agricultural economy anywhere in the oriental world that would permit entry of the occidental trader. There began a slow and transitional shift in the nature of agricultural production-exchange throughout the oriental world.

As European traders began purchasing teas and silks in China, the village farming communities responded, although economic historians have made much more of the issues of the inadequate responses. As Japan later opened up her tea growers to foreign trade, they enlarged their plantings in order to satisfy the European market, and as occidental buyers shifted their purchases of silk to Japan, the Japanese farmer increased his mulberry plantings. As American traders in the late nineteenth century began buying coconut and abaca in the Philippines, village agriculturists responded by increasing their plantings. As the Malays and Indonesians gradually recovered from their reactions to European plantation development, they began planting a few coffee bushes and rubber trees among the jungle-like village gardens, fitting them into an already complex plant ecology. Throughout the whole of the oriental world slight shifts in planting patterns did little to change the gross appearance of regional landscapes, but these shifts subtly began to alter the nature of regional production systems by producing or increasing volumes of particular commodities beyond the levels needed in traditional supply. And late in the nineteenth century as the deltas of the Irrawaddy, Chao Phraya, and Mekong rivers came into agricultural development, through the development of flood control systems, the traditional wet-field rice system regional surpluses developed that began to flow to those regions in which the plantation systems were provoking food deficits. Ceylon, Malaysia, and Indonesia became steady rice importers in consequence of their plantation developments. India's cotton and wheat exports needed compensation by large rice imports. Japan, in her emphasis upon industrialization in new urban population clusters, became a food deficit region, adding to the interregional movement in food products. After about 1875 China became a food importer, and by the late 1890's the Philippines no longer was feeding itself adequately. These small shifts in regional patterns of production began to affect the nature of local economy, develop interregional exchanges of food volumes within the oriental world, and develop regular sources for those commodities of interest in the occidental world.

As the shifts in agricultural production began and as occidental trader demands steadily grew, there also began changes in internal economic structures throughout the oriental world, for classes of wholesalers-dealers, millers-processors, middlemen-commission agents evolved to handle the transfers between village producers and occidental exporters. This has been best described for China as the growth of the compradore system, but its equivalent institutional element appeared everywhere. In Burma-India-Ceylon Indians chiefly handled things, but for China, the Philippines, Vietnam, Cambodia, Thailand, Malaysia, and Indonesia the Chinese took over the roles involved. In Korea and Japan the Japanese were the operating element. These new institutional structures stood between the traditional rural village community and the large port cities where the occidental trading communities became centered. In mainland southeast Asia and in the island world where native entrepreneurial initiative seemed unresponsive, the Chinese have long been accused of dominating commercial enterprise. In the contemporary period since independence came to the colonial lands the Chinese have been subject to restrictive controls in the various national efforts to promote economic nationalism.

Throughout the whole oriental world this slow transitional shift in agricultural economies has continued to the end that there are few regions that do not participate to some degree in the cash economy aspects of regional development. To this extent the traditional peasant economies described earlier in this chapter are undergoing evolutionary development. The degree of participation varies markedly within countries and regions, of course. The integral shifting-cultivator societies, attempting to maintain their traditional living systems, do not markedly participate. The peasant agricultural communities still located far from transport routes cannot participate significantly in regard to primary crops since these will not stand the friction-of-distance costs of transport.

Those regions not yet well serviced by internal transport remain more regionally self-operative than regions well served by mass transport facilities. But as transport facilities expand into regional hinterlands more and more village communities are being drawn into the patterns of cash economy and commercial production. In many formerly traditional village communities the entry of commercial agriculture is having strong repercussions on social structure, regional mobility of families, local political organization, and other aspects of village life.

Regionally, there are short-term variations and interruptions in what is a long-term general trend. Thus, in Burma the restrictions placed upon the Indian wholesalers-dealers-moneylenders caused their emigration back to India. Since the late 1950's Burma has been in a state of relative hermitage that may or may not be starting to lift in 1973. Nationalization programs, the decline of rice production, and the restrictions on foreign contacts caused the near cessation of the rice export trade, and the future of Burma's participation in the world of commercial exchange is in some doubt. The decline in administrative efficiency in Indonesia after the mid-1950's both strangled the developing patterns of trade throughout the whole of Indonesia and promoted widespread smuggling of particular products out of western Indonesia that strongly upset and unbalanced the normal systems of interregional exchange. The nationalization of the economic systems of North Korea, China, and North Vietnam has at least temporarily altered the systems and flow patterns of both internal and external economic exchange, and the military turbulence of South Vienam has totally upset the evolving economic structures of that region. There well may be other serious variations and short-term imbalances created in regional exchange systems throughout the oriental world before the several national politico-economic systems achieve long-term stability.

In the growing changes that have taken place in the agricultural economies of the separate regions on the oriental world, and despite the continuance of the plantation systems of production, it remains true that the peasant smallholder is producing the largest volumes of commercial products that enter interregional and international exchange. And it assuredly is true that the traditional peasant village agricultural system everywhere is in transition. Where nationalization programs have dominated the restructuring of regional systems the aspects of change are, of course, far-reaching in extent and go far beyond the agricultural systems as such. It remains true, however, that there are just too many peasant agriculturists in the whole of the oriental world putting too much pressure on the land. Since the pressure of too many peasant agriculturists exerts strong pressures on the whole of the cultural systems involved, the oriental world is subject to many other kinds of far-reaching cultural change. It is an open question whether or not changes in land tenures, productive technologies, economic structurings, social reorganizations, and political administrations can come rapidly enough to prevent drastic turmoil to the non-Communist portions of the Orient. Only in Japan, so far, is there clear assurance that the traditionl oriental agricultural world has been satisfactorily metamorphosed.

CHAPTER 5

the east, the west, and modernization

The occidental folk myth of the unchanging East is one of the most pervasive perception pictures of the modern world and is about as incorrect as the oriental folk myth that all Americans are rich. There is a fundamental difference between the elements of continuity and integrity inherent in a culture system and the aspects of temporal change that occur over time within that culture system. Every operating society attempts to maintain its own inherent integrity, but no society permanently can avoid processes of temporal and secular culture change over a long period of time. Occidentals often have mistaken the issues in their subjective reactions and considerations of societies in the oriental world. Any careful reading of the history of any oriental society lays the fiction of the lack of change but strengthens the conclusion that there is continuity to the culture stream within any oriental society that achieved such spatial dimensions, and such cultural strength, as to form a persistent regional society. The policy makers of early Han China must have thought that they were establishing a system of societal operation that could function in perpetuity in about the same way that the founding fathers of American society believed that they were establishing a system operable in perpetuity. That the Han Chinese succeeded in articulating a basic system that held up for two thousand years is a credit to their skills and abilities, but that the basics of the system continued operative does not negate the processes and aspects of change that came into that system and that were blended into the web of Chinese life during the long period. The Chinese conceptual view of the world, and the Chinese definition of Chineseness, remained true to the early formulations, the Chinese peasant villager maintained his close symbiotic relation to his land, rural folk religion remained the earthy pragmatic system of its progenitors, and Chinese architecture held to its elements of continuity.

87

Such varied elements of continuity suggest that there is the same kind of intrinsic integrity to Chinese culture that French or British Europeans point to with pride in respect to their own national cultures.

Much depends on how one approaches the issues of culture change in the assertion of "unchanging," the label which the West has attached to the East. There are those, for example, who make much of the un-changing nature of the French rural farmer, even to the use of the term peasant in describing his psychology, and there often is the implication that the peasant continuity is one that has characterized rural France for well over a millennium. Certainly one receives impressions of unchang-ingness when reading about the quality of certain French wines, since one speaks of traditional methods in the vineyards, the processing sys-tems, the cellars, and the human producers. The Chinese became tea drinkers long before the British, but one of the elements of continuity for the British way of life often is held to be the afternoon tea habit and the cup of English tea. That the peoples of the Orient persisted in their opposition to European overtures, pressures, and militant conquests, ef-forts designed to facilitate European commercial prosperity, cannot legiti-mately be held as proving that orientals are unchanging. That the Japanese persisted in maintaining their own control of the complex aspects of industrialization, declining to grant territorial and economic concessions to Europe, while modernizing their economic system, cannot be asserted as unchanging.

A primary aspect of the European view of the unchangingness of the East has had to do with the matter that the East did not respond to the early overtures of the West in the ways that the West desired. The sheer persistence of the West in attempting to make the East react in the approved manner has its own elements of unchangingness. As a well-educated Chinese once remarked to me: "The first Europeans to come to China acted like barbarians, and too many Europeans still come to China acting like barbarians." Both the views of the East and those of the West have always been developed through subjective reaction systems as par-ticular forms of perception.

The animistic peoples of Indonesia accepted many of the new ele-ments of Indian culture that were brought to them before the start of the Christian Era, they later accepted much of the new Islamic way of life, and they have accepted much of the European systems of culture, and none of these suggests simple unchangingness. That the Japanese tribal groups of the pre-Christian Era reordered their whole cultural system after examination of the Chinese model and that they have again reordered many aspects of that system in becoming an industrialized and urban society suggest that the Japanese can and do change when they see justification for change. That the West eventually utilized such things as vaccination, coal in the form of coke, the casting of iron, hormone extracts derived from particular animal sources, and paper and printing, all first developed in China, suggests only that the peoples of the West also were amenable to change when the opportunities occurred and the justifications became clear. Each set of issues must be considered on its own terms, for both East and West.

There is clear evidence that, in A.D. 1500, in manufacturing technologies related to consumers goods of most types, several oriental regional centers were more advanced than any region in the West. The cotton textiles of southern India were then the world's best, the silks of southern China and Japan were well in advance of any textiles of Europe, the porcelain industries of China and Japan were far above the pottery of northwestern Europe, the gold, silver, and brass work in decorative jewelry and art pieces of varied motifs were as good or better than anything out of the West, and the sea-going Chinese shipping could outsail European craft both in the technical sense and as volume cargo carriers. In several regions of the Orient the well-to-do and wealthy lived in luxury patterns that, in terms of what western economists sometimes call conspicuous consumption, probably exceeded anything in the West of that day. There were more wealth and productive capacity in the large populations of several regional centers in the oriental world than were present in all of Europe of that day. It is probably equally true, however, that the poorest of the poor in both realms lived close to the meaner margins of existence, with little choice between them. And the Orient of that day had many more small culture groups living in fragmented regions under very simple systems of culture than was true in Europe of that day.

There is ample ground for the conclusion that, out of the inter-regional contact of East and West, the West reacted more forcefully and more rapidly in respect to processes of culture change. The currents of culture change in the West had already begun stirring and simmering and, after effective sampling of the life of the East, those processes of culture change in the West came to the boiling level. The East, on the other hand, long used to trade contacts between regional centers of the oriental world and going through patterns of regional change within the oriental world at the time, reacted indifferently or negatively (Fig. 14). On the one hand there was confidence in the integrity of their own culture system, as in the case of China, an expression of superiority toward barbarian overtures. On the other hand the negative reactions of Korea and Japan were marked, resulting in the shutting off of all possible contacts. In southern and southeastern Asia, portions of the oriental world that were in politico-cultural flux, reactions were fragmented, contradictory, and piecemeal in terms of local regions, and somewhat militant in the traditional pattern of the Mediterranean Basin kind of conflict—Christendom *versus* Islam. In sum, modernization really began in the materially ambitious West and made its most rapid and marked progress there. The piecemeal, indifferent, or superior reactions of the oriental world did not then stimulate the processes of culture change in the same ways, on the same levels, or at the same rates. To this extent the East soon became a lagging zone in which certain kinds of change did not proceed rapidly and were not equivalent to those kinds of change taking place in the West. There were many kinds of change going on in the East, after A.D. 1500, but those changes were often not obvious to Europeans, they did not improve political strength, they did not increase military technology, and they did not immediately lead to the accumula-

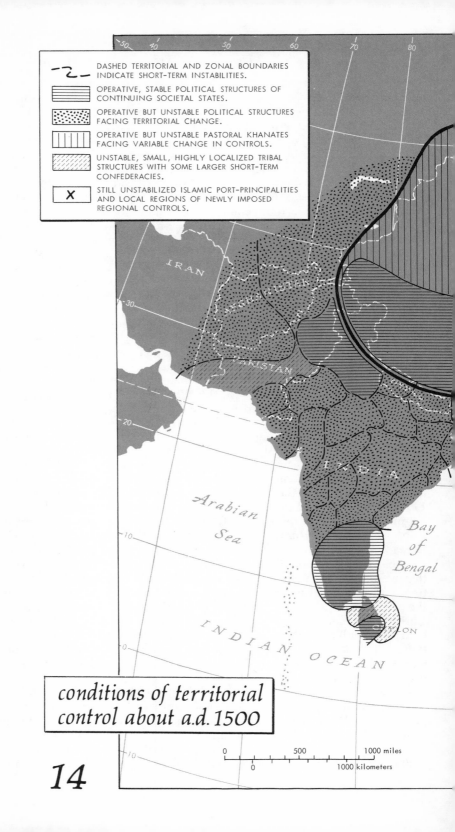

IRAN

AFGHANISTAN

PAKISTAN

INDIA

Arabian

Sea

Bay
of
Bengal

CEYLON

INDIAN   OCEAN

*conditions of territorial
control about a.d. 1500*

14

0		500		1000 miles
0				1000 kilometers

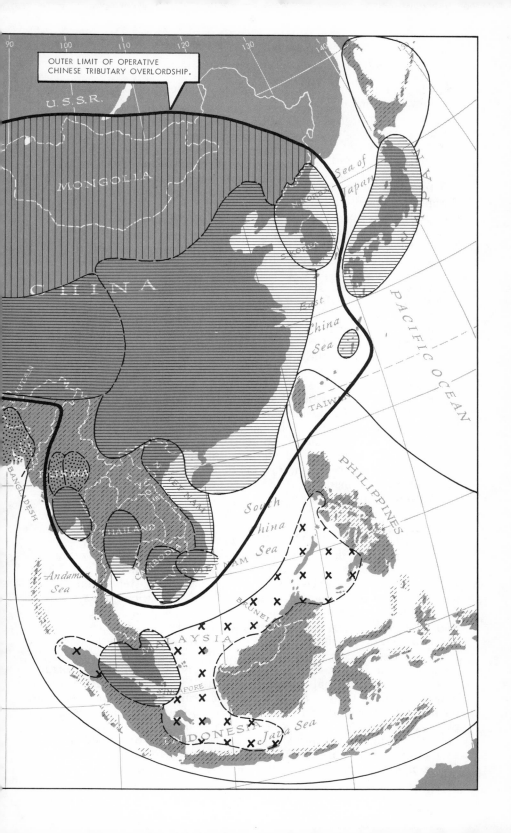

OUTER LIMIT OF OPERATIVE
CHINESE TRIBUTARY OVERLORDSHIP.

tion of capital resources invested in the development of an industrial complex based upon power resources.

The modernization of culture systems, in renovation of old technological systems, into new concepts of political territorialism and into new economic systems began first in Europe, accompanied by a new kind of aggressiveness, and around this conceptualism of modernization there is no question that Europe led the way and that the oriental world lagged and then suffered from its indifferent, negative, and restrictive policies. European ships became floating gunnery mounts that, coupled with European aggressiveness, achieved dominant control of the oriental seas and shipping routes. The Chinese reacted negatively, their ships no longer being frequently seen in Indian ports. Arab traders fought back in their own way for a time, but they could not match the European advances in militant protest or in shipbuilding because they had no organized government support behind them. Europeans introduced new spatial dimensions to the patterns of interregional trade which no oriental trading system could match. The modernized concept of one trading world, as an earth-wide linkage, was both alien to the oriental world and beyond its field of interest. Oriental concerns essentially had been agrarian, localized in the sense of regional living systems, and inward looking in terms of continuities, and no oriental society conceived of the retaliatory kinds of measures that could have redressed the balance— measures such as attacking European ports and demanding territorial concessions within European states. Whetted by their findings, supported by their successes in world linkage, and utilizing several technologies derived from the East, Europe launched into what we now term modernization via the Industrial Revolution. But culture change in numerous ways began taking place throughout the Orient in the seventeenth century to begin the manifold kinds of changes that have become cumulative within the oriental world.

Change in Agrarian Economy

By A.D. 1500 almost all crop plants utilized anywhere within the oriental world had been tried out in about every other region of that world. Although changes continued in planting systems and in the gradual expansion of the cultivated landscape, the agricultural systems of the Orient had been well stabilized at an earlier period. The introduction of American crop plants into the oriental world first came in the sixteenth century in the Philippines and in India. From these centers of dissemination American crop plants slowly became diffused all over the oriental world, finding their ecological zones of adaptability and integration into the traditional cropping systems. Significant results followed upon such adaptations in many regions, affecting the agricultural systems, changing land use, altering dietary systems, and producing changes in population densities within local regions. Thus, for example, the sweet potato was introduced into the southeastern coastal provinces of China by Chinese trading in the Philippines. The sweet potato spread all over China, finding its most satisfactory home in the Szechwan Basin of west

China where it became a primary crop on the upper, dry terrace lands that could not well be put into wet-field rice. A bountiful producer, the sweet potato became an integral crop in a complex rotation system throughout the basin, markedly increasing the total food supply, becoming the base staple at the lower levels of food pricing, and becoming a factor in the modern increase of regional population. The sweet potato is cultivated almost all over China today, except in the far north. In the far north, central, and northern Manchuria, the white or "Irish" potato found a significant place in the short-season cropping systems and, in the twentieth century, has become a staple cash-sale and food crop.

In the Philippines, under Spanish urging, Filipino shifting cultivators moved from their straggly littoral barrios into "pueblos" and became sedentary agricultural farmers cultivating both native and American crops. Previously growing a little rice by shifting-cultivation techniques in the near-shore zones and maintaining small village gardens, Filipinos became sedentary farmers who have expanded their cultivated landscape over the major land portion of the islands. But rice never has yielded well in the drier central section, the central and western Visayan Islands. Here, about 1800, American maize caught on as a basic food staple and the crop has expanded in acreage ever since to the end that the maize landscape of the Philippines is one of the primary elements. In the process of their settling down in sedentary villages the Filipinos became thoroughly Hispanicized and controlled their own domestic politico-social system under the cover of Spanish hegemony. In the processes of acculturation the Filipinos remained an agrarian people, but they became the one Christian nation in the Orient. More recently Americanized in social and economic culture, the Filipinos took to commercial agriculture as smallholders, chiefly producing significant export volumes of sugar, coconut products, and abaca, largely oriented to a favored American market. Although cane growing is largely a smallholder operation under contract to the sugar miller, the pattern requires concentration of cane fields around and within access of the sugar "central"; therefore, the cane landscape is a restricted one. Stimulated by the American market for coconut products, on the other hand, the smallholder is gradually spreading the coconut landscape over the central-southern Philippines and replacing the original tropical forest cover.

The settlement and agricultural development of the great deltas of mainland southeastern Asia (the Ganges, the Irrawaddy, the Chao Phraya, and the Mekong) are other phases of the shifts in agrarian life. Relatively empty in the pre-European era, drainage and canalizing of the wet deltas permitted the expansion of the cultivated landscapes of these particular portions of the Orient in significant fashion. Such expansion has provided significant shares of participation in the commercial economy of the oriental world through the production of jute (Ganges Delta) and rice as export crops, but it also has built up dense population clusters that stand out on the population map.

A lesser illustration of the kinds of change in agrarian economy relates to the west coast of India. The cashew nut tree was introduced into western India from Brazil, probably by the Portuguese in the sixteenth century, and along the humid coast south of Bombay the tree found an ecologically adaptable home to the extent that it soon spread through the forest cover of the noncultivated lands. More recently a garden-orchard crop tree, but also gathered wild from the forest, the cashew nut has become an important regional item in commercial agriculture, and the west coast of India is the chief producer of cocktail-party cashew nuts for the world today.

Another significant aspect of change in agrarian life relates to the decline of the agrarian Japanese population. Long omitted from the program of modernization in Japan, agriculture in the period since World War II has seen the steady decline of the traditional rural Japanese farm family. Small power equipment and electric power for some jobs have been the agencies of small-scale industrialization of Japanese agriculture. Almost all farm families now have members participating in off-farm economic pursuits, many farm families are but part-time farmers, agricultural production is greater than ever before, and the strictly agrarian labor force has dropped to a low level. Few other oriental societies can, to date, absorb the agrarian population surplus in the way in which Japan has done, but this remains the goal of many programs of industrialization.

A last consideration of an aspect of agrarian change in the oriental world relates to the complementary position of handicraft manufacturing. The early pattern was one in which local regions all over the oriental world carried on varied patterns of local production of consumers goods as an auxiliary or ancillary system in the utilization of surplus labor supplies not seasonally occupied in the primary crop-producing activities. There were, of course, both regional and "national" specializations that moved both within discrete societal bounds and also between countries within the oriental world, but the overriding aspect was that of basic regional self-sufficiency. There were also variations in the level to which manufacturing had developed, with the Philippines operating at a very low level, whereas both India and China carried on rather sophisticated activities. Earliest European trade ventures had little of manufactures to sell that could compete, but as the nineteenth-century European industrial plant matured its whole range of products, now high in quality, began attracting consumers throughout the oriental world. There then followed the steady decline in oriental handicraft manufacturing. The agrarian impact of this decline was to force rural populations into further dependence upon primary agricultural production at a time when European urban industry was beginning to absorb rural surplus populations and labor supplies.

Underemployment within the agrarian structure of the oriental world is not the traditional feature that modern economists make it out at all, but it is a product of the nineteenth and twentieth centuries in which the urban industrial plant of the West has forced the rural handicraft plant of the East into liquidation. The result has been the serious underemployment problem among the rural agrarian peasantry throughout the oriental world, producing a declining level of living for those populations. Only Japan has so far managed to break the enervating cycle of downward trends in levels of living, though other portions of the oriental world now are engaged in upward trending "economic development" in a struggle to break the cycle.

This conflict in economic production systems can, of course, be viewed as purposeful economic imperialism and proponents of the conviction that the West is purposefully evil in intent make what they can of it. It would appear equally valid, however, to view such patterns in terms of the essential elements of evolutionary change in human culture on a world-wide basis. The shift from rural agrarian-handicraft socio-economic structures to urbanized structures employing industrial procedures both in manufacturing and in primary agricultural production is a basic shift similar to that achieved when "civilization" created the city and the political state or to that achieved when Neolithic crop-animal production replaced Paleolithic collecting economies. If such evolutionary change in world culture is a sin, then the West must continue to bear that cross. That the East has finally accepted much of industrial orientation and is attempting to accommodate to such cultural change means that the economies of most eastern societies will go through evolutionary change on whatever basis each society within the oriental world can utilize, whether it be that of the Communist world or that of the neo-capitalist world. In respect to the traditional rural agrarian orientation, the oriental world is rapidly changing, with rates that vary from that of Japan to those lesser rates operable today in Thailand or East Pakistan.

Indicated in a previous chapter was the rising importance of the smallholder in the commercial economy of the modern era, as related to the agrarian sector. This is one part of a basic shift in the nature of regional production systems, in that local and regional self-sufficiency is declining steadily. To date, of course, the shift has not become sufficiently efficient to strongly elevate the levels of rural living, for many of the socio-economic adjustments to commercial economies have not been integrated into the economies of many of the oriental countries. Effective commercial economy implies adequate transport between hinterlands and centers of commerce, effective financial institutions which bring commercial transactions to every producing unit in terms compatible to modern commerce, information concerning markets and guidance facilities regarding agricultural technology, and education of the rural productive population to the levels at which they can utilize all the elements of the commercial economic system. Nowhere in the oriental world is this integration complete, although Japan is approaching it and Taiwan is well on the way.

That mainland China now claims that wheeled vehicular transport reaches every county seat among the more than 2,000 counties (*hsien*) suggests a great advance over the conditions of a century ago when wheat or rice transport was limited to roughly a fifty mile movement in the hilly country of southwest China by its human-porter transport costs, but that is only a beginning. That export rice (basically a very cheap commodity in farmer returns) from central northern Thailand reaches its port of export at all is a credit to the native organization of traditional transport on the Menam Chao Phraya, but for such a cheap product to benefit the level of living of rural Thai peasant farmers requires highly efficient volume transport, storage, and national financial institutions. That Burma's nationalization of agricultural land was an attempt to reduce the control of the moneylender indicates an effort to break the traditional structure which held the rural peasant in bondage, but that its development of government corporations to handle commerce has yielded a very inefficient "modernization" is clearly shown by the very marked decline in the export of rice. Both moves, together, have almost taken Burma out of the rice export trade, its chief source of financial return from participation in the commercial world. That millions of peasant farmers in India, Pakistan, and Bangladesh still must depend on the same sort of transport system that served Mother India two thousand years ago, the ox cart operating over unimproved dusty or muddy rural "tracks," suggests that the smallholder participates in the modern system of commercial economy under very strong handicaps. Some thousands of Indian villages today can be reached by institutions, facilities, and procedures that are modernizing the agrarian scene, but they still are outnumbered by those for which modernization still is not available.

There is no question but that the winds of change are blowing in every country in the oriental world and that close-in hinterlands are shifting out of their traditional systems in every aspect of life, but very widely there still is the reaction of the rural populace that ". . .those things cannot operate here, still."

Resources, Their Appraisal and Usage

The oriental world, in a sense, evolved to a mature level as a set of cultural systems chiefly concerned with the organic world made manifest by nature. In the common oriental view of nature those living things such as trees, flowering plants, four-footed animals, birds, and man composed the living environment. Water, air, and fire are among the natural elements, and so is the earth in the direct sense, all conceived as positive and negative in variable manifestation, active as parts of that living environment. Metal occupies an anomalous position, being one of the essential elements in some oriental views of nature but never permitted to assume an artificial position as a positive economic component since it was not in the same sense an active element in the organic world. Man could use all the elements of the organic world, but he was beholden to nature and to the gods, he was a creature of that living world, and it was not his right to tamper too greatly with the harmonics of nature by prying into or disturbing the earth too greatly or by altering the nature of materials too greatly. This did not at all prevent the resculpturing of agricultural surfaces into terraced fields on which to grow crops since wild plants and trees quickly clothed the margins of such surfaces with their tolerated wild growth in a restoration of the manifest natural world. Nor did the view of nature restrict the building of dikes along rivers in floodplains or the digging of canals into the lowland surfaces, for waters could still flow, active and operative within the natural world. Trees could be cut for fuel or construction, clay could be baked into utensils and bricks, stone could be quarried and cut for use in monumental building, in roads, or in other natural uses, and nature soon clothed the human scars and constructed manifestations with its own living marks to rectify these slight intrusions into the natural world.

The transformation of ores into metals and the fabrication of metals into humanly conceived products altered the intrinsic nature of things. This could be tolerated to the level of producing the minimal variety of utensils, tools, and weapons suitable to the carrying on of the simple agrarian life, but it could not be carried too far. Among philosophers alchemy was always of interest and was widely practiced, but the interest was intellectual and metaphysical, quite unrelated to the practical concerns of the artisan-tinkerer who dirtied his hands and body grubbing in the earth, working around hot kilns and over hotter furnaces, manufacturing utensils, tools, weapons, and the minimal range of economic materials needed by any human society. Although the master craftsmen who designed and finished the decorations of many of the finer goods for royalty were honored, the ordinary artisan's rank in the social structures of the oriental world was a relatively low one, and societal policies on the exploitation of natural resources were controlled by philosophers and scholars at a much higher social level, so that no premium ever could be placed on inventiveness, material technology, or the value of mineral resources as agencies of economic development. Among the upper classes there were always those few individuals interested in the practical applications of scientific engineering principles, and their insights did lead to a great many technological beginnings, particularly in China, but in general religious philosophers and political administrators saw implications of corruption of the natural world, the agrarian orientation, and the simple natural life in such things, so that policy decisions were always such as to prevent the rise of technological development above the level at which there were provided the material necessities of the simple agrarian living system for the masses of the population in every society in the oriental world.

Since royalty, being related to the gods in the oriental view, always were entitled to the finest products that human skill could provide, the uppermost political classes always enjoyed both the services of their peoples and the ample supply of fine quality goods, but even here the range of technologies remained limited to those that provided the kinds of things utilized by the lower ranks of any society. There was much variation, of course, in levels of technology and in levels of socio-political organization among the peoples of the oriental world. The simpler cultures produced simple tools, utensils, and decorative things that could be exchanged with peoples of higher levels for some of the products not internally fabricated. The levels of technology in many aspects were far higher in China than in the Philippines, but internally the same relative systems operated in the Philippines as in China, tribal chiefs having the best things that could be provided by the limited artisanry of Filipinos. In that at various times both Indian and Chinese rulers held hegemony over wider regions, the flow of tribute goods from the lesser societies brought products from far places to both Indian and Chinese imperial courts, complemented by the return flow of the finer goods from these higher technologies. But throughout the whole of the oriental world the scale of economic development remained consistent with the view of nature.

This controlled state of affairs remained in operation when the Europeans first came East. The range of things that interested Europeans in the East was regionally quite variable, of course. Natural product spices of the Indies, the textiles, brass work, art goods and some spices of India, and the teas, silks, lacquers, wood carvings, ivories, and copper wares of China provided a large range and volume of things "new" to the European. The various oriental societal groups declined to alter their views of nature, to upset their natural living systems, to produce beyond the levels at which life could continue within the construct of their natural worlds. Within that construct the peoples of the oriental world had long been familiar with almost all the common minerals, precious and semi-precious stones, woods, oils, essences, gums, resins, and other extracts of the organic world. The sources for such were known, the production patterns were adequate to the normal oriental patterns of use. Although data are not adequate to construct production curves or flow-of-trade tables, it is clear that the artisans of the oriental world maintained their supplies of raw materials in sequences in order to maintain the handicraft manufacturing system. The production of iron ore in China was sufficient to yield something near 100,000 tons of iron products per year in the early nineteenth century, for example, a volume quite adequate to the simple agrarian-economy demands that were in tune with the cultural system.

As the European Industrial Revolution achieved its early mature strength, and as both political and industrial pressures began to bear down on the oriental world, there slowly came about a pattern of change in the thinking about the nature of the world among the leaders of those societies that suffered the greater pressures. Advocacy of European industrial technologies began, but policy decisions were slow to change with regard to implementation. Europeans began establishing processing facilities for agricultural products of interest to Europe and then began establishing factories for the fabrication of some of the simpler products, the outturn destined both for oriental markets and markets outside the Orient. It was only when such undertakings trained native labor in new skills and provided on-the-ground examples of western technology that a kind of sense of inevitability ensued, leading then to the first oriental adaptations of the European industrial system. In India, China, Indochina, and the Indies Europeans had begun the industrialization of the oriental world without the acquiescence of that world. This was one result of European economic imperialism, and it was most effective in those regions in which political controls were most effective. As such there is ground for the assertion that political and economic colonialism and/or imperialism entails a training procedure of some significant value in the process of economic development.

Japan, of course, provides an example of an alternate route to economic development. The Japanese view of the world had been essentially similar to that of other parts of the Orient, and the Japanese came late to the awareness of the intrinsic nature of European industrialism. But with sudden awareness came sudden change in economic policy decision-making, so that Japanese industrialization was a national effort both sanctioned by and led by government policy decisions. At every step since the 1860's Japanese national economic policy has led, supported, and financed the reconstitution of the Japanese economy, unlike the routine showing up elsewhere.

Slow as it has been in many parts of the oriental world, the shift in outlook toward the physical world, the material earth, and the utilization of resources has been pronounced. Industrialization is the goal of every oriental national society, in some degree. Those lands least exposed to the "training procedures" have been slowest in development, i.e., Thailand, Cambodia, Laos, and South Vietnam, although Ceylon is not much more advanced either in technology or in outlook. Korea came late into the training ordeal, but under Japanese control a great deal of training occurred at the lower levels, Korean management skills being least developed of all, since Japanese controls restricted the levels of Korean participation in industrial management.

The outlook for material resources has gone through considerable change in the last century and a half. Europeans were first impressed by the range of economic resources and by the relative frequency of presence in the marketplace. With the onset of industrial beginnings, however, the volumes of known resources seemed rather small in comparison to those known elsewhere, and small in comparison to the demands of the new industrialism, and the future prospects were written down. But now that orientals are interested in material resources in the industrial sense and have started examining their own territorial ranges in detail the volumes seem far more adequate in many respects than once was the judgement. As recently as twenty years ago Thailand was considered to be a portion of the earth with almost no mineral resources other than a little tin and tungsten. The picture now looks much less bleak, although Thailand's mineral resource volume will probably not turn out to be the "veritable storehouse" that belongs to China. Not all countries within the oriental world have all they need for domestic economic development, but it is too early to make flat predictions. Again, Japan may be an exception in that the range of resources is very great but the volume in any one seems rather small particularly when the industrial plant has been built to the capacity that it has.

The oriental world has altered its view of the earth in large degree, but how completely has that view been altered? There are many leftover and lagging viewpoints, and there is a residue of older attitudes. Even thoroughly trained "industrialists" exhibit ambivalence in attitudes, demonstrating one view at their place of business and another at home. Philosophically, the East has accepted many of the views of the West, but there remains the integration of these contrasting views both in terms of national policy and in terms of personal thought systems on the parts of the individuals who make up oriental society in any one country. It is too soon to say what will be the oriental attitude toward the earth in the twenty-first century.

And for all that the attitudes toward the earth and its resources have been infected with the viewpoints and objectives of the West, only in Japan has industrial achievement so far provided the mass of any population with very many annual quotas of industrial goods derived from exploitation of resources in the modern manner. Even in Japan the industrializations of the last century has gone primarily into building up the industrial plant and paying for the import of resources through exportation. Chinese villagers relish the new flashlights, bicycles, tools, and other simple fabrications that are now becoming available from Chinese industrialization, but the first fruits of industrialization must be devoted to producers goods, capital equipment in the way of plant and primary transport system, and the consumers goods come later in the sequence. Similarly, in Thailand or the Philippines the establishment of the industrial base has so far utilized the great share of resource development, and the change in economic philosophy has not yet significantly affected daily living systems in rural villages. The distribution of consumer goods requires a degree of maturity through time that does not yet appear anywhere except in Japan.

Cities, Urbanism, and Urbanization

The city and urbanism were not invented or concocted in the oriental world in the modern sense of that regional distinction but originated just to the west of the modern Orient. However, both cities and urbanism have long been part of the culture systems of the oriental world, but both remained conceived as in the earliest constructs, and it is the West that has redefined the city, urbanism, and the cultural functions pertaining thereto. The city was first conceived as a temporal and religious center in which the symbolism of political administration was combined with earthly administration of religious affairs on behalf of the gods. The ruler of the state was both god and king, and the city embodied those physical manifestations appropriate to each in the temples, palaces, treasuries, religious monuments, workshops and barracks, shrines and sacred places. As such the city was the center of culture, the seat of power, the functional heart of the state. The ruler performed both temporal duties by setting forth the law, by allocating land and resources, and by administering justice, and he performed religious duties by performing the appropriate rites at the proper seasons on behalf of all members of the state. In the original construct there perhaps was just one city to each state, and the city was the embodiment of that state.

As states expanded in spatial form it became necessary in some cases to establish at varying distances secondary settlements that embodied the representational functions of the ruler because transport and communications technology could not then overcome the friction of distance. It has been customary to treat these secondary settlements as the headquarters of feudal lords and lieutenants in the purely temporal sense of military and political power, but each also became a subordinate center for the exercise of religious rites and, conceptually, the subordinate settlement was the extension of the full-bodied function of the state. As such the subordinate settlements were more than places of residence and, there-fore, held status of a sort quite different from the residential villages in which ordinary citizens made their homes.

In the early constructs of the ancient city that have remained to the present there are evidences of the palaces, treasuries, workshops, temples, shrines, and sites for the exercise of rites, but the architectures of the homes and shops of the main populations have all disappeared. The purely secular life of the ancient state is hard to plot because the remain-ing artifacts are but broken bits of things, and there is little evidence remaining as to where the mass of the population lived and the kinds of houses in which they lived and worked. But obviously the housing of the mass of the population need not be constructed in the same manner as the monumental architecture that embodied the conceptual construct of the state, and domestic architecture involved perishable materials from nature befitting the simple life of the agrarian peasantry.

These basic patterns of contrast between the city as an embodiment of the state and the secular urbanism that surrounded the city remain into modern time in the oriental city not yet strongly affected by con-cepts out of the West. Urban geographers have repeatedly pointed out the contrast between the size of "the city" and the size of other settle-ments throughout a given state. They have pointed out the patterns of formal planning and architecture that have characterized "the capital," along with the contrast in functions between the capital and other settle-ments. Bangkok, in Thailand, probably was the last native founding of an imperial capital in the classical manner, in the late eighteenth century. There had been earlier Thai capitals, of course, embodying the same kinds of features that were built into Bangkok, and the contrasts between the capital and the subordinate settlements always were great. But western scholars have often overlooked the complementary role of the subordinate settlement and, looking at size alone, have sometimes as-serted that there were no other urban settlements than the capital in some of the countries of the oriental world.

In the oriental world there has always been a clear distinction be-tween the "city" as an urban place and the "town," "market center," or village. Size, morphology, the amount of trade flow, and the diversity of manufacturing are not the critical elements. Such elements rested in political administrative functions and in the functions of religious per-formance, the role of culture, and the practice of those arts that pertain to the regional system of culture. But they also rest in the conceptual control of the societal system as a whole, for the city is the repository of the functional heart of the culture. The urban geographers of the West, secularized and conceiving of cities as economic entities with particular morphologies and diverse functions, have largely missed this aspect of urbanism in their mapping, counting, enumerating, and ranking.

Urbanism, in the classical and older oriental sense, lay in the simple gathering together into cities sufficient numbers of people of sufficient variety of learning to perform the chief functions of the culture system. Artisans of many kinds always were involved, but so were artistic crafts-men, poets, philosophers, those learned in the law, bureaucrats, administrators, priests and other religious practitioners, sages, and keepers of the rites. In the capital more of all of these were needed than in the subordinate center, but in the latter kind of settlement there were enough of each to carry on the cultural system and to ensure its maintenance. A population containing these elements comprised an urban settlement, a city. Lesser settlements might include more traders, purely utilitarian artisans, those engaged in processing agricultural produce, transporters, and merchants. In that all settlements needed contact with the regional cultural stream there were shrines and priests in all towns and market centers, and so on, but the distinction between the "city" and the residential "village" of the rural hinterland was clear. Religious pilgrimage from lesser settlements to cities or particular sacred places was a part of the cultural system, and the nonurban populace participated to the degree that it could and felt the cultural call.

After the West, with its concerns for trade, industry, secularizing of political influences, and its emphasis upon ports as "points of contact" between West and East came into the oriental world, the oriental conceptual structure of the state, the capital, and the city slowly began to change. Warehouses, "factories," "labor forces," and "economics of the marketplace" impinged upon the several oriental cultural systems, and port facilities, systems of customs control, land transport, territorial "peace and order" suitable to international trade became issues between East and West, as the West pushed its efforts at trade. Slowly there began an urbanization process, as the chief ports and other points of contact for trade demanded more and more services of a kind never critical to the older oriental city or capital, causing the cities to grow even faster than the regional rates of population increase. The capitals in due course approached the "million" class in those areas in which capitals were the points of contact. In other situations old villages were picked by Europeans as points of contact, and huge agglomerations of people accrued. The case of Calcutta is a prime illustration of the village site chosen for the European founding of a secularized agglomeration of people brought together to serve the new patterns of international trade. In classical terms Calcutta was but a rural village, remote from a center of culture, and the European creation of a large settlement classified as a port city by European standards and criteria has created one of the greater slums of the earth.

Shanghai was at least a minor regional city under the traditional Chinese system when the Europeans picked it as a point of contact. Its conversion into a great trade and manufacturing center was accompanied, in some views, by its decline into a sinkhole of political and moral iniquity at the height of European influence, and Shanghai has never completely recovered. Shanghai ranks high among the cities of the world by European criteria, but it has constituted a special problem case in the modern era. Because the Chinese now have adopted the conceptual structuring of trade and manufacture, in terms of locational strategy and the practical use of industrial beginnings, Shanghai continues to grow as a great center of trade and industry under Communist management, but Shanghai remains a special problem case in cultural control even now.

Peiping (Peking) never became an economic point of contact as did Shanghai and Calcutta, and its relationships centered around political linkage between the East and West. Peiping has now been converted, in part, into the super-metropolitan district that goes with modern industrial urbanization but, in part, the Chinese have tried to maintain the aura of the great capital in the massive reconstruction of the heart of the city as a place in which to conduct the rites that give sanctity to the state in both the temporal and the mystical. And in the world of the West, too, there is the modern effort to create something of the cultural core to the city, to relieve the drabness that goes with purely secular expansion of the "marketplace" concept. The distinction, in the West, of the Great City, as opposed to the city, is an expression of this cultural symbolism.

As the population has grown throughout the oriental world, in many places overreaching the amount of land that can be put into agrarian systems of production, both urbanism and urbanization have increased. The subdivision of older and larger units of territorial administration has created additional cities within the last few centuries, settlements that are sometimes hybrid forms of the classical city and the modern market-place. The trend toward subdivision is old, but the hybridization process has affected only the last three centuries of development. And increasingly the acceptance of the concept of the industrial settlement has created new kinds of cities throughout the oriental world, characterized by large factory establishments and dormitory communities of a sort somewhat alien to the concept of the urban entity in classical oriental terms. Although Ranchi, in the Chota Nagpur hill country of India, is an old city now undergoing hybridization in its expansion, Jamshedpur, as the site of the largest iron-steel complex in the Commonwealth, is a modern kind of settlement producing many dollars worth of product but engendering little true development of culture in the true sense. And though Paotou, in North China, has been converted from an old caravan terminal marketplace into a heavy iron and steel center, the Chinese have not yet done much to lift the level of its cultural soul to the level necessary to create a true city. In modern terms both Jamshedpur and Paotou are cities, but in classical terms they are but marketplaces; whether or not they are cities in cultural terms can be questioned.

As the contrast has grown between the rural peasant agrarian living systems and the modern industrial system of the marketplace settlement, and as socio-political and economic-industrial change continues to increase its tempo, the obvious contrasts in the material aspects of living systems are altering the perception-values among the rural populations throughout the whole of the oriental world to the end that urbanization, in its technical modern sense, is outrunning urbanism in its classical cultural sense. Floods of rural inhabitants are beginning to pour into cities where populations have freedom of movement. (Within the Communist world people try to make the move, only to be moved back periodically into the rural scene by government pressure under various pretexts usually linked to such phrases as "improving the conditions of the rural masses.") Calcutta continues to increase in size, although its death rate currently is higher than its birth rate. Although the percentages of urbanization for the whole of the oriental world are not yet so striking as those in many parts of the West, the oriental world is coming to have more large "cities" than the West, and the process is only getting under way.

Again, Japan seems to be an exception to what is happening elsewhere in the oriental world, but one can wonder whether or not this really is true. Japan has now passed the threshold level in urbanization, and more people live in "cities" than in rural areas. The nature of the physical environment is a factor of course, but the acceptance of the concept of modernization-industrialization has been more fully executed in Japan than in other portions of the oriental world. The Japanese have been able in many ways to retain a cultural contact with nature, even in their urbanizing, and they currently are reacting strongly to several issues of the problems of the marketplace, e.g., air and water pollution. However, the central portions of many of the largest and most modernized Japanese cities are coming to resemble the same sectors of the cities of the West more and more, with many of the attendant problems, and it remains to be seen whether or not the Japanese can modernize their cities without overdoing the westernization of the urban scene.

Modernization, Westernization, Economic Development?

In common with much of the non-West throughout the world, the oriental world's leaders were, at one point, tremendously impressed by the apparent military and economic strengths of the countries of the West, and they were impressed by the apparent superiority of western systems of transport and industrial technology. At the same time they were dismayed by the aggressiveness of that West and by the ideologies displayed by the political systems of that West. Alteration of some aspects of the conceptual concepts of society and society's aims and procedures obviously was required. Renovation of the conceptual structures became thought of as modernization, but it also became thought of as westernization. Modernization-westernization became a symbolic concept by which to alter the classical ideologies, conceptual structures, and operating systems throughout the oriental world, with time differentials in separate societies as to when the inevitability of such became accepted. Westernization loosely became a synonym for modernization in many minds. More recently the concept of economic development has come into usage as particularly referring to some aspects of the process of cultural change in the non-West. And sometimes economic development is taken as a full synonym for both modernization and westernization, as though all three processes meant the same thing in respect to cultural change. In casual usage all of these separate processes do involve and invoke something of industrialization in the sense of applying new technologies to the utilization of natural resources for the betterment of levels of living. But some of the processes require far more than others, and in reality the three terms are not at all synonyms.

Economic development properly refers to the maximization of material production-distribution-consumption systems within a society.

Westernization properly refers to the cultural acceptance of the material and nonmaterial culture of the West, and it obviously implies economic development within value systems of the type common in the West, but at the same time it implies something of secularization in cultural terms. Modernization, on the other hand, implies reconstruction of classical conceptual systems, in any society, compatible with the circumstances to be faced, internally and externally, by which to maintain societal integrity on all fronts, economic, cultural, and political. Modernization may reject selected aspects of westernization, but modernization must come to terms with problems of economic development in some compatible way if it is to succeed. Since being faced with the dilemmas imposed by the linkage of the whole earth into one transport and communication system, no society can permanently maintain an isolated existence untouched, or unaffected, by actions, events, and consequences of an external nature. Therefore, every society on our earth desiring to maintain its intrinsic integrity must now undergo something of continuing cultural change through time. The attitudes toward such cultural change are in good part determinants of the rates of change and the kinds of change, but these are determined by the sum total of societal perception and determination. Leadership can enhance or restrain rates, patterns, societal perceptions, and the processes of cultural change.

Japan is a prime example on both ends of the problem. Shortly after A.D. 1600 Japanese leadership sought to hibernate from the outside world, and that leadership largely succeeded for over two hundred years, although processes of cultural change continued to develop slowly in internal and domestic fields. In the 1860's, faced with a display of development in the outside world, Japanese leadership reversed its stand and took Japan on a program of cultural change that altered Japanese society in fundamental terms at a set of rates rarely seen in world history. What the Japanese did was to modernize their whole set of conceptual structures for the operation of society within a conceptual system still compatible with Japanese culture. This modernization took the form of westernization in many specific ways, but there was strong selectivity to it all, and the Japanese rejected many aspects of westernization because some of the items were not compatible with the Japanese cultural system. For example, in economic development terms the Japanese did not do away with all small units of economic production, so that even today the largest number of "manufacturing establishments" employs so small a number of workers that economists find this a contradiction to the economic theory of industrialization. That most Japanese personnel remain with the same firm lifelong does not accord with economic theory in the West, but it is compatible with Japanese socioeconomic concepts. That agriculture for long was left to lag well behind industry in "modernization" was sometimes taken as a misunderstanding by the Japanese of the processes of economic development. However, that planned lag kept the rural populations gainfully and busily employed until such time as the maturing of urban industry could effectively absorb the increased labor force and provide the right kinds of equipment to modernize and semi-mechanize the agricultural system. Currently the labor force employed in agriculture is at a very low level, but Japanese industrial agriculture is not yet going in the direction of a few huge farms, state or private, but remains in the hands of small operators who often are part-time farmers. In the technical sense Japan has sought economic development, and modernization, with selective westernization when that was compatible with programs of modernization that could maintain the integrity of the Japanese culture system. Japan, clearly, is the best illustration of successful selective cultural change within the oriental world, but the processes have not yet run full course and some problems remain.

Elsewhere in the oriental world there are cases that demonstrate quite different aspects of cultural change. Certain phases and segments of westernization have been perceived as valuable, and these remain goals of modernization, with programs being put into force as rapidly as economic controls will permit. Industrialization remains a general aim for most portions of the oriental world, although the elements are quite variably envisioned (Fig. 15). Other aspects of westernization are in conflict with elements of the societal culture systems and there develop indecision, beginnings that are then cut off, tangential implementation, and what appears to be confusion and inefficiency. Still other aspects of westernization are being variably rejected, although the struggle for modernization continues. Many of the aspects of modernization raise basic questions about the directional evolutionary change within the culture system concerned. What the West often takes either for unwillingness to change or for oriental inefficiency is really the result of inability to make changes rapidly that are compatible to societal objectives as perceived by the mass of the population involved. Far too much stress has been laid on political issues and on the sheer matter of economic progress, as defined in the West, and far too little appreciation for the matter of societal goals as perceived through the eyes of the population involved.

In an earlier chapter the comment was made that when the Burmese drove out the Indian moneylender class and when the farmland was nationalized, there was considerable inefficiency resulting, to the end that Burma may never again be an important rice exporter. The gaining of foreign exchange by commercial export through which to purchase abroad material equipment for the uplift of the material level of living is a goal perceivable and compatible with the conceptual system of the West, but whether or not this becomes a long-term and high-ranking goal of the Burmese may be an open question. The inefficiency of Burmese economics is very great in western eyes, but economic efficiency does not yet seem to rate very high on the list of goals for the Burmese themselves. One may always question whether or not societal leaders interpret and express the will of the population, but it is very clear that the Burmese find many matters of westernization incompatible with important aims, structures, and conceptual frameworks within Burmese culture.

At a superficial examination it may seem that Singapore, in taking to urban industrialization so fully, has sold out to westernization, and it may seem that Thailand simply is refusing to change significantly with its very limited program of economic development. Both societies are being buffeted by external winds that exert pressures internally, but Singapore's leadership is working at the issues of cultural compatibility in industrialization-modernization, and Thailand's program appears to operate within a controlling system that relates strongly to the cultural system of the Thai. In the long-term view Thailand is going through modernization compatible with its cultural system, whether or not its rates of change, and the forms of change, appear productive to the West.

China appears, since 1949, to have gone through revolutionary change of a sort totally inconsistent with its cultural system. In a sense this is true, since 2,000 years ago China opted for the agrarian society against the industrial society, but by 1850 China had come to the end of an era by running out of farmland on which to maintain its agrarian living system. However, in its recent program of revolutionary change there is copious evidence that the new cultural forms are being adapted to fundamental cultural controls intrinsic to Chinese culture. Two decades is far too short a time in which to judge the revolution within a cultural system, and the world will need to wait another half century, at least, to determine the degree to which Chinese culture has succeeded in achieving a modernization compatible with basic Chinese conceptual demands.

On the Indian subcontinent leadership is struggling with the issues in a context that seeks modernization without revolution. Both India and Pakistan opted for industrialization within the prevailing basic structure, but in India the pattern is less conventionally out of the West than in Pakistan for there are more issues of socio-cultural incompatibility to be solved. Modernization in India still faces some of the most severe economic and cultural problems within the oriental world, and there remains division of opinion on whether or not this can be accomplished without a much more painful form of revolution in conceptual and organizational systems. (Here the term "revolution" is used in the strict sense and not in the loose sense of the *coup d'etat* that brings a shift among the holders of military-political power.) Pakistan assayed the modern political state under unusual difficulties; that it did not succeed is in part owing to the sheer costs of modernization and in part to the unwillingness of the West Pakistan rulers to spread the investments in modernization into the East Pakistan segment of the then operating state. This means, of course, that the new state of Bangladesh commences its independence under extraordinary circumstances of financial poverty and political pressure. The ultimate structures of the now separate states of Pakistan and Bangladesh are not clear at this writing, and their cultural directions and developmental programs are subject to great handicaps and heavy pressures.

The processes of cultural change have been in motion throughout the oriental world during the last century. Slowly here, rapidly there, wholesale in this society, piecemeal in that society, rather smoothly in another, with what seems to the West utter confusion in another case, but always in progress. To the impatient observer from the West the patterns, the rates, the signs of progress, and the marketplace elements seem both inefficient and frustrating. However, oriental peoples are

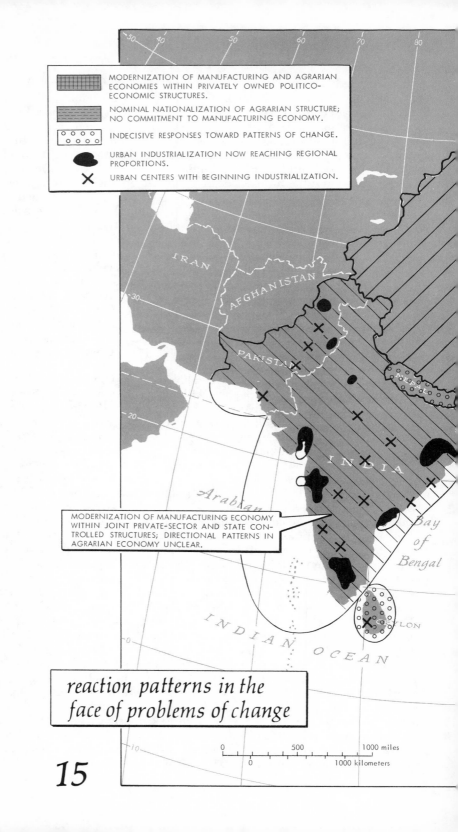

MODERNIZATION OF MANUFACTURING AND AGRARIAN ECONOMIES WITHIN PRIVATELY OWNED POLITICO-ECONOMIC STRUCTURES.

NOMINAL NATIONALIZATION OF AGRARIAN STRUCTURE; NO COMMITMENT TO MANUFACTURING ECONOMY.

INDECISIVE RESPONSES TOWARD PATTERNS OF CHANGE.

URBAN INDUSTRIALIZATION NOW REACHING REGIONAL PROPORTIONS.

× URBAN CENTERS WITH BEGINNING INDUSTRIALIZATION.

MODERNIZATION OF MANUFACTURING ECONOMY WITHIN JOINT PRIVATE-SECTOR AND STATE CONTROLLED STRUCTURES; DIRECTIONAL PATTERNS IN AGRARIAN ECONOMY UNCLEAR.

reaction patterns in the face of problems of change

15

0   500   1000 miles

0   1000 kilometers

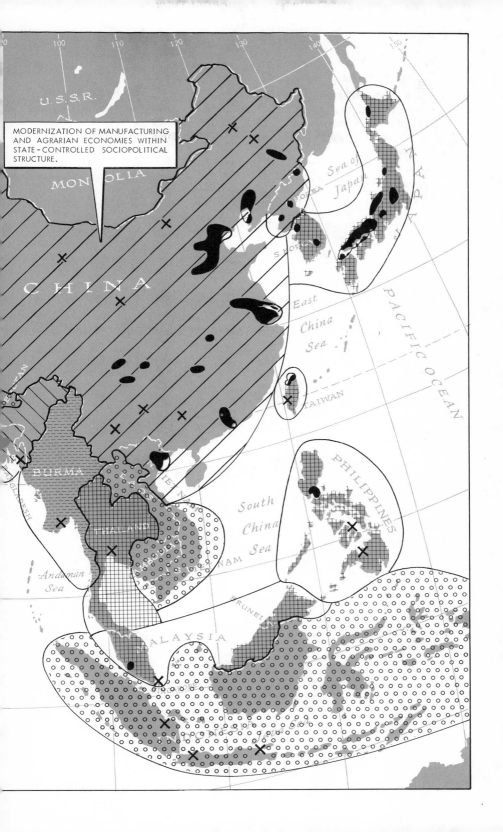

MODERNIZATION OF MANUFACTURING
AND AGRARIAN ECONOMIES WITHIN
STATE-CONTROLLED SOCIOPOLITICAL
STRUCTURE.

picking and choosing, hesitantly taking some steps and boldly taking others, and the historiography of cultural change in the oriental world may record perhaps another full century of continuing change before degrees of completeness appear to have been achieved. Patience is called for, as the West should have learned in its earlier effort to remold the East.

CHAPTER 6 *crises, dilemmas, and alternate possibilities*

At the height of each regional movement fomented to throw off the occidental colonial controls of the last few centuries, each society in the oriental world put forward some such expression as: "We would rather be free and poor, to face our crises in our own way." The Philippines was the one partial exception to this, since independence had been promised and was openly given in 1945 (formal inauguration in 1946), as the first release from colonial control. For over two decades the oriental world has been free of colonial controls, but free of imperial responsibility also, and crises have come to each and every country. Each country, including those that never suffered outright colonial control, now faces a series of dilemmas in which it appears that in no single country is there fully unified agreement on what is the proper course for that society. Perhaps Japan, again, is an exception, but even here there are problems of future policy that must be faced. The disagreements over future developmental policies, cultural directions, and socio-economic practices have ranged from local riot to national rebellion, from starry-eyed idealism to downright chauvinism, from retreat from facing problems to outright demands for international aid in reconstruction of the systems of culture. The manipulation of power in ruthless enforcement of change has taken millions of lives so far, and a sober but still nonbloodthirsty projection of future prospects envisions the disheartening prospect of more millions dying in violent disagreement, at the very least.

The growth of colonial empires in the oriental world was both slow and uneven (Fig. 16). Japan, Korea, and Thailand never were parts of any occidental colonial empire, although the peoples of all three had variable amounts of contact with occidentals. China never lost her own sovereignty, although she was subjected to trade treaties granting rights that occidentals took full advantage of. And China was pressured into granting not only special privilege (extraterritoriality) to occidentals but also territorial concessions in many port cities over which China had no power at all. India (the whole subcontinental, traditional area) was haphazardly compartmented in respect to the degree to which British administration came to bear on local regional development, some areas receiving strong imprints and others but token impacts. In sum, however, occidental colonial empires did not blanket the whole of the oriental world, even though the repute of such did spread through the whole territory.

The occidental world, today beset with its own problems of culture change, often expresses dismay over the long continuance of disturbed conditions in the now independent oriental world, conditions that range from mere agrarian unrest to violent and militant struggle. However, in certain respects the problems of contemporary culture change throughout the oriental world are of greater magnitude and are more fundamental than any problems that have arisen in about two thousand years of oriental life, and they will not be disposed of quickly or easily. These problems involve not only the internal identity and life style of individual societies, but they also involve accommodation to the rest of the earth and its culture systems in a way never before required. The solutions to the various societal problems of the oriental world will take time and effort, and they will demand the utmost patience from the rest of the earth.

The Crises: Recapitulation

The primary crisis is that of population. The totals are too high, the growth rates are too high, the demands for living space are too great for accommodation in most portions of the oriental world today. *Of course* there are local regions of low density, *of course* some of the regional densities are less than those of some parts of the occidental world, and *of course* there still are a few areas of reserve, and there are areas amenable to agricultural modernization in the sense that this means lands susceptible to mechanized operation as that term is understood in the United States (Fig. 17). The aim of the oriental world, however, is to lift the levels of living and not merely to fill out the remaining lightly populated or empty spaces with the same kinds of densities and low levels of living that already exist in the more heavily populated sectors. The comparison of regional densities with portions of the occidental world is an idle illusion, for the economies, societal structures, and levels of living do not all compare.

Having accepted such culture institutions as the public-health services, much of "western medicine," new patterns of control over water systems, and the discard of infanticide, the oriental world has found its families burgeoning out of control as the birth rates have soared and the death rates have dropped to a startlingly low level. The rates of natural increase are threatening for the future in the face of too great numbers already living. Accommodation to patterns of low rates of natural increase requires basic change in social mores in every country in the oriental world to the end that they also require revision in traditional conceptual principles.

Although there are programs of population control in several oriental countries, Japan is the only national society (so far) able to carry out an effective control program. Since 1948 Japan has pursued a goal of reducing her rates of annual natural increase to a level compatible with levels of growth in economic development, so that the national level of living has been climbing steadily. The Japanese natural increase in population now stands at slightly over one million per year, and popular acceptance of the concept of population control suggests that Japan now can maintain control of future rates of increase. No other country now is able to implement so effective a national population control policy, although North Korea and mainland China probably could do so if such a policy could be squared with Communist philosophy. In both North Vietnam and South Vietnam the question of population policy cannot be faced squarely because of the military circumstances. In every other country the population problem remains in crisis condition, since no other regional administration has the administrative strength, technical means, or popular support to mount a really effective campaign of population control.

A second crisis, following out of the initial problem, relates to the agrarian structure of all parts of the oriental world except Japan. In all other countries if the recent migrants to cities, the rural landless, and the tenants having too little land were to be moved, instantly and without cost, onto existing reserves of economically usable agricultural lands, there would not be enough land to go around, today, let alone to provide open lands for the agrarian populations coming of age in the next few years. The agrarian crisis is not simply a case of landlordism-tenancy, although this is the issue so often trumpeted by the radical. The basic fact is that the oriental world is facing the exhaustion of reserves of good, arable, problem-free agricultural lands. Allowing that the above move cannot be effected, it is common to state that there are small reserves of good land in every country, but that the exhaustion date is not far off, the actual prospective date varying from country to country. In fact, however, such countries as South Korea, China, and possibly India, began using problem ridden marginal lands decades ago. In every country there are reserves of land, but this is marginal land with a degree of marginality so strong in some cases that there do not exist the capital resources and the engineering means to bring these lands within the range of profitable agricultural utilization in traditional terms. Many such lands lie in hilly to mountainous country presently not served by basic elements of transport or the other facilities that are necessary to permit populations of poor either to get to them or to begin their development. Other such lands face serious problems of flood control, drought control, soil erosion in the past, soil salinity, or simply soils so poor that costly build-up procedures are needed.

Agrarian reform, meaning some procedure of converting tenants into owners-operators of the lands that are now tilled by debt-bound tenants, is often held to be a solution to the agrarian crisis. The time is too late

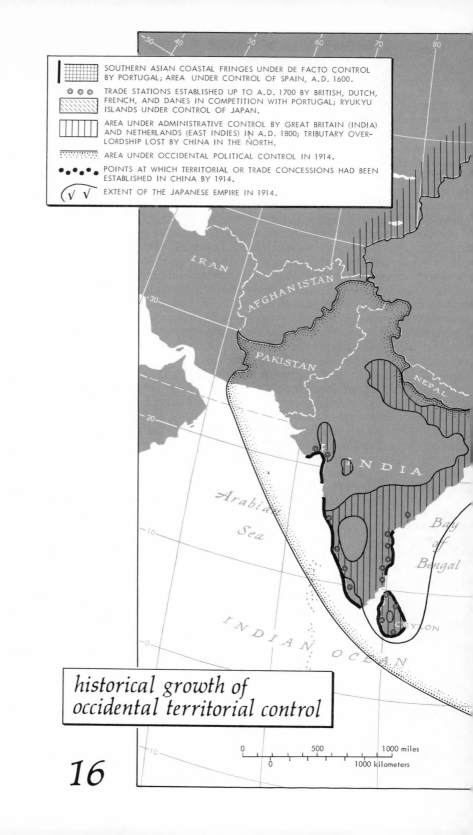

SOUTHERN ASIAN COASTAL FRINGES UNDER DE FACTO CONTROL BY PORTUGAL; AREA UNDER CONTROL OF SPAIN, A.D. 1600.

TRADE STATIONS ESTABLISHED UP TO A.D. 1700 BY BRITISH, DUTCH, FRENCH, AND DANES IN COMPETITION WITH PORTUGAL; RYUKYU ISLANDS UNDER CONTROL OF JAPAN.

AREA UNDER ADMINISTRATIVE CONTROL BY GREAT BRITAIN (INDIA) AND NETHERLANDS (EAST INDIES) IN A.D. 1800; TRIBUTARY OVER-LORDSHIP LOST BY CHINA IN THE NORTH.

AREA UNDER OCCIDENTAL POLITICAL CONTROL IN 1914.

POINTS AT WHICH TERRITORIAL OR TRADE CONCESSIONS HAD BEEN ESTABLISHED IN CHINA BY 1914.

EXTENT OF THE JAPANESE EMPIRE IN 1914.

IRAN

AFGHANISTAN

PAKISTAN

NEPAL

INDIA

Arabian Sea

Bay of Bengal

CEYLON

INDIAN OCEAN

historical growth of occidental territorial control

16

| 0 | 500 | 1000 miles |

| 0 | | 1000 kilometers |

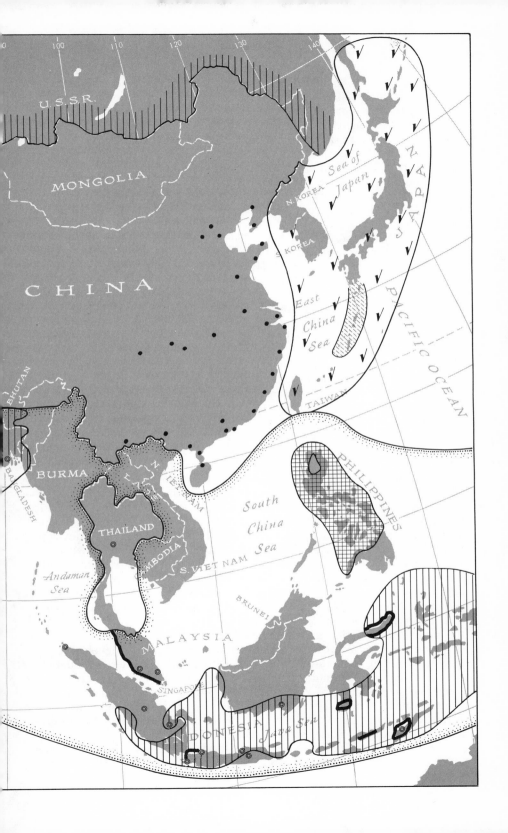

for such a solution to be adequate if the level of living of the agrarian populace is to be lifted above the peasant level. The consolidation of fragmented farm plots is often advanced as another drastic need in many portions of the oriental world to permit efficient operation of agricultural endeavors. Peasant farmers often have opposed such programs, since it would remove the flexibility inherent in different soil conditions which permit production of different kinds of crops. Consolidation of farmlands would be productive of increased efficiencies were the whole farming systems to be altered toward modernized agricultural systems, but simple consolidation under peasant socio-economic structures is not an adequate answer in today's world.

China, North Korea, and North Vietnam, under Communist controls, have been through basic agrarian reform programs that liquidated tenancy and that effected consolidation of fragmented holdings, and each of the three programs has clearly demonstrated the basic fact that there simply were too many people trying to live on the land and from the land. In a few areas of favorable landscapes and agrarian conditions China has established large mechanized state farms that can approach modern industrial agricultural operations, but for the most part all three countries continue a labor-intensive variety of agricultural system that is closer to peasant systems that to modern agriculture at its best.

A third crisis must be stated in economic terms, for it concerns problems of national capital accumulation in societies in which the mass of the populations both are poor in capital resources and have little cultural incentive toward the compounding and focussing of capital resources in modern terms. In economic terms the primary economic good has been seen as the complex of land, homestead work animals, tools, and such "property" as was culturally defined in the various regional societies, to the perpetuation of peasant family living systems in the agrarian scene. Transforming the rural agrarian society into something else, however defined, requires the reorientation of the economic systems and the painful extraction of capital resources by small accumulations that can be made applicable to modernizing programs of development. By whatever means, Communist or capitalist, this is a slow process when even the "wealthy" members of each society have previously subscribed to the same kinds of concepts of wealth, economic investment, and use of resources. Outside the Communist world, wherein ruthless programs operated, there are few effective mechanisms at the disposal of a society, its leadership, or the political state by which to bring about the rapid accumulation and mobilization of capital resources.

Applications of outside capital resources, through developmental loans or foreign economic investment in material resources production, run both risks in economic terms and the politically loaded problems of economic neocolonialism. Without adequate controls the infusion of large sums of money can become diverted into less than developmental programs, as has occurred. The majority of the large sums paid the Philippines by the United States after World War II went into consumer goods rather than into programs of economic development, and the use of loan funds in Indonesia during the Soekarno era contributed little that was truly developmental. Outside capital resources, applied through the Colombo Plan by Commonwealth nations, United States aid programs, recent Japanese aid programs, and corporate investment programs have infused, probably, larger amounts of capital resources into portions of the oriental world than have been applied from domestic sources in those countries outside the Communist realm. United Nations programs have been able to bring forth a larger relative share of domestic capital application in particular ways, but the total problem remains a serious one.

Somewhat related to the above condition of crisis is the general matter of financial solvency of the several state systems, particularly in South and Southeast Asia. Built into the traditional political structures and operating systems of the oriental world have been peculiar systems of financing government administration. It is only in the modern occident that there is fairly efficient significance to Benjamin Franklin's phrase about the certainty of death and taxes. Tax administration throughout the oriental world always has been subject to vagaries, exceptions, irregularities, inefficiencies, and incompletenesses. Modern government structures have not been able to install the relative efficiency of taxation considered as operative and mandatory in the Occident, and a problem critical to the strength of the political state is its inability to fund its own operations effectively. Coupled into this aspect of strength of the state, in financial terms, has been the holdover element from traditional political structures that involves the state bureaucracy, in which a considerable share of the state resources go to supporting an over-large government establishment. The Communist states of North Korea, China, and North Vietnam have restructured their government tax systems in comprehensive terms, but it is not clear if any of the three systems really functions efficiently.

A final crisis relates to the nature of government itself. Every political state in the oriental world, except Japan and Thailand, has a governmental system put together since World War II, but even Japan and Thailand show elements of change in the structure and operation of government during the post-war period. All of these new government structures involve components out of the past and members of bureaucracies steeped in the several systems of culture, even as they involve new structures and new conceptual principles. It is clear to the objective view that the peoples of the oriental world view governmental problems, policies, and practices from different points of view, but it is equally clear that nowhere in the oriental world is there total commitment to any single conceptual principle by which to structure a governmental system. Although the occidental observer totally committed to what he envisions as efficient, democratic, representative government can point out conceptual contradictions and operating inefficiencies (somewhat in the sense of some of the problems itemized in previous paragraphs), the contradictions and inefficiencies often do not appear in that same light to many in the oriental world. Nationalism in the oriental world today is spatial, but it is also cultural, religious, psychological, and of mixed historic-modern institutionalisms. In many of the oriental societies there are educated members who have had exposure to the full range of con-

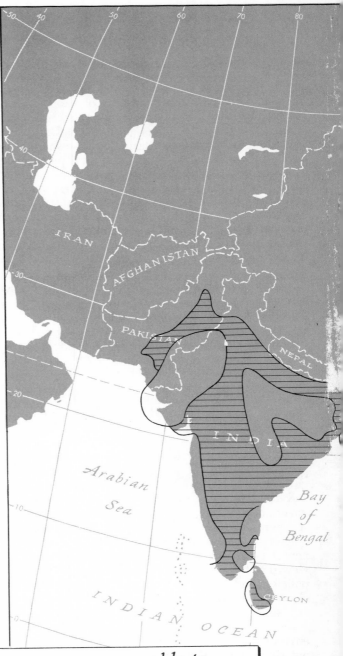

chief large areas amenable to
efficient agricultural modernization

0   500   1000 miles
0   1000 kilometers

17

ceptual principles by which government can operate today. Retaining elements of anti-Western feeling, many among the several leaderships see their societal futures in ways difficult for an occidental to understand. The compromises implicit in operative political systems do not appear to them to pose the simple dichotomy so often framed by the advocate of communism *versus* democracy.

In the activist sense a great share of the population of the oriental world still is not vitally interested in the structuring of large-scale instruments such as national governments, retaining the traditional view of the peasantry concerned with the local village community "world" and putting up with the thrust of political power from outside that "world" as best they can under pressure. In historic terms it seems fairly evident that the peasantry would purposefully opt for Communist governmental structuring, but their political response remains relatively passive toward the national issue, as such. In China the peasantry responded to those who promised solutions to local problems of land, taxation, and the impact of local officialdom without concern for the national structure in specific political terms, yet the response of the peasantry was critical to that political decision. Everywhere in the oriental world, except for Japan, there remains a peasantry heavily burdened by the pressures of the national governmental structure, whatever that may be. That nowhere in the non-Communist sector of the oriental world has the operative structure of government satisfied the localized concern of the peasantry remains an ominous threat to the future structuring of government.

The issue is still joined in the two Vietnams in 1972, with no solution immediately evident. This is not the place appropriate to a full discussion of either the Vietnam problem or the problems of government structure elsewhere in the oriental world, and no such will be attempted. It is clear, however, that no really satisfactory structuring of modernized government has found a final and firm acceptance in any country of the oriental world, including the Communist bloc. In several of the countries that structuring, and consequent operation, has been so indecisive that some form of military control of government currently operates. In 1972 one may place South Korea, Taiwan, Indonesia, Burma, Thailand, Pakistan, and the Philippines in this category in factual terms. Currently, the Philippines, Malaysia, and Singapore *appear* to operate under civil government systems not in immediate danger of military takeover, but neither of the structures is beyond contest, since there are socio-economic problems in each not currently in the process of demonstrably successful solution. India stands at a crossroads, for it is a country that is conceptually committed to nonviolence but engages in a variety of militant endeavors while engaged in a competitive campaign for further internal change. Within China the general structure of government appears not to be in question, but the specific internal structure, and the role of bureaucracy, remains strongly in question in respect to the interplay between national and local governments.

The nature of government, and the nature of the relations of government to local populations, remains in flux everywhere in the oriental world, even in Japan. The day has passed in which national government may rest lightly upon local regions, border zones, and ethnic societies, upon local economies, ethnic living systems, and minority groups, but in no one society has a totally successful modern system matured. For Japan the issues may seem relatively minor, but Japan's new position in an industrial world poses some problems of internal nature that are not yet rationalized. Elsewhere, the search is for the basic structural elements that may be worked into effective institutional patterns that resolve both the problems of the local "world" and the modern national political state. Until these problems are resolved in the relatively distant future, the oriental world will remain in a state of crisis, impending or actual.

Dilemmas: Assessment

For each country of the oriental world the issues of accommodation to the rest of the earth in contemporary time involve four sorts of problems, but the urgency of each of these varies according to the cultural perception of the rest of the world by the individual society (Fig. 18). The following paragraphs do not follow precisely the fourfold pattern laid out in Figure 18, but they do range around the general theme. There are four problem zones that can be stated broadly as: (1) Relative status position as a cultural-political power, (2) restoration/establishment of an economic system providing an adequate level of living for the population involved, (3) establishment/re-establishment of a regional spatial identity compatible with the modern concept of the national political state, and (4) restoration/achievement of a stable nation-cultural identity in a competitive world. Each of these problem zones constitutes a complex of subproblems around which there focus matters of national cultural attitude on the one hand and practical matters of determining strategy and operational tactics on the other hand. Each, in a sense, involves determination of the goal to be sought and the practical procedures by which to achieve that goal.

The above statement infers that one can assume that a spatially distributed population does somehow possess a societal unity sufficiently cohesive, and sufficiently steeped in societal mores, that leadership can both formulate satisfactory programmatic policies and can detect what should be the objectives in those programs. This is the heart of the dilemma facing leadership in the several societies of the contemporary oriental world. In some cases the task does seem to be one of carrying out the program, but in others the real crux of the dilemma seems to lie more in the zone of determination of an identity (cultural, political, economic) that can be furthered in spatial and operational terms. Here one cannot make simple generalizations for the whole of the oriental world, since the particular aspects of the problem group vary for each regional entity that the earth recognizes today as a "political state." For example, Laos and China stand at different positions with regard to each of the four problem zones, just as Bhutan and Japan face quite different aspects of the same four problems.

If one considers China's approach to the issues of accommodation, he can understand much of what goes on and why China took the position

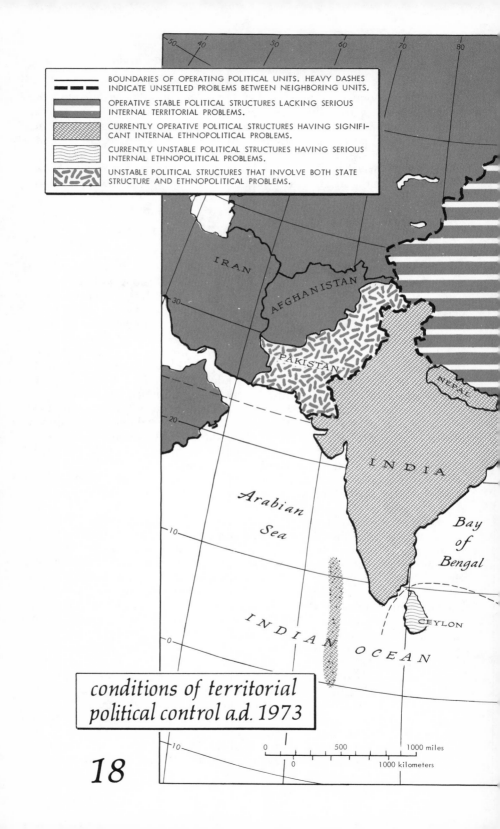

BOUNDARIES OF OPERATING POLITICAL UNITS. HEAVY DASHES INDICATE UNSETTLED PROBLEMS BETWEEN NEIGHBORING UNITS.

OPERATIVE STABLE POLITICAL STRUCTURES LACKING SERIOUS INTERNAL TERRITORIAL PROBLEMS.

CURRENTLY OPERATIVE POLITICAL STRUCTURES HAVING SIGNIFICANT INTERNAL ETHNOPOLITICAL PROBLEMS.

CURRENTLY UNSTABLE POLITICAL STRUCTURES HAVING SERIOUS INTERNAL ETHNOPOLITICAL PROBLEMS.

UNSTABLE POLITICAL STRUCTURES THAT INVOLVE BOTH STATE STRUCTURE AND ETHNOPOLITICAL PROBLEMS.

IRAN

AFGHANISTAN

PAKISTAN

NEPAL

INDIA

Arabian Sea

Bay of Bengal

INDIAN OCEAN

CEYLON

conditions of territorial political control a.d. 1973

18

| 0 | | 500 | | 1000 miles |

| 0 | | | 1000 kilometers |

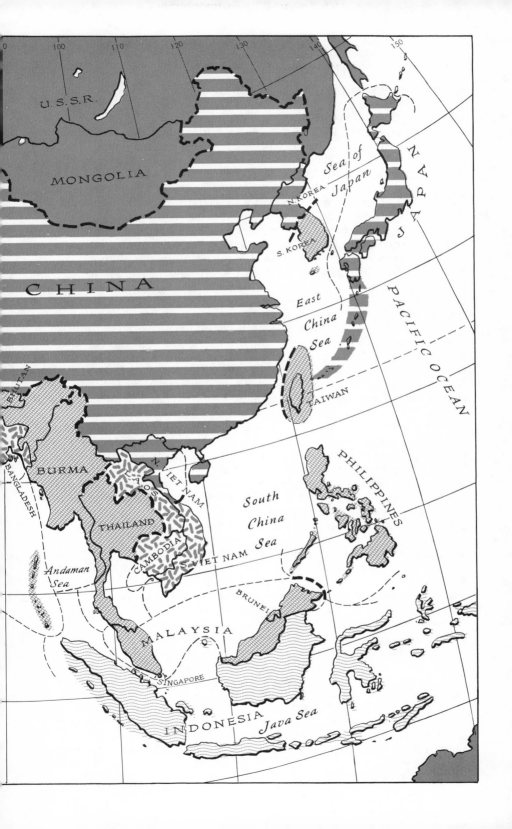

she did, by reference to the four-problem complex. China, long used to the position of being cultural and political superior, still smarts under the indignities suffered in the last four hundred years (indignities both subjectively perceived and real), and a critical issue in accommodation to the modern world is that of restoring her position as one of the great superiors of the earth. Political invective heaped upon those countries adjudged to be leaders/competitors is merely part of the operational program designed to restore that superior position. The Maoist restatement of the conceived eternal verities of Marxism-Leninism, and the tiffs with the USSR over such matters, is also part of the program. The land reform/collectivist trend in agriculture and the forced pace of aspects of industrialization are operational elements in renovating the outworn economic system. Squabbling over boundary problems with every surrounding political entity except North Korea and North Vietnam is the operational tactic of solidifying the spatial dimensions of the political state as demanded by political mapping of such things in the current world, and of bringing to world notice the specific limits of that state. The internal cultural gyrations (often considered so strange, bizarre, or contradictory by outsiders), e.g., the treatment of minorities, the Cultural Revolution of 1968–1970, the various programs of "do's" and "anti's," and the unceasing "struggle" sessions are all concerned with the redefinition of "Chineseness" in the modern world, consequent upon the purposeful destruction of certain old elements after the Communist assumption of power.

China is obviously making headway in her problems of accommodation to the modern world, and the rest of the world is revising its opinion of China. Chinese persevered at research and operations to the end that China joined the somewhat exclusive "nuclear club" able to orbit ballistic missiles and rockets. Purely military defense? That might be, but its status element is consonant with Chinese aims. Chinese aggression in Tibet has been roundly denounced, but the map of political China is being clarified in the political atlases of the rest of the earth. Exorcised by much of the world for brutal reorganization of the agricultural economy and the system of individual rights, China has developed a form of mobilization of labor in the domestic economy that, combined with a strict consumer rationing system, provides fairly adequately for all but the outright rebellious. Similarly exorcised by world aid programs China has mounted an industrialization that has moved further than thought possible two decades ago. Often described as culturally schizophrenic in its several "cultural" revolutionary programs, China has clearly succeeded in some aspects of establishment of cultural mores that create a new China, but one consonant with eternal Chineseness. Issues, problems, difficulties and uncertainties remain to be dealt with, including the problems related to too many people, but political-economic-social-"Chinese" China is more fully integrated as a regional and cultural entity today than it has been for well over a century. The territory of China was a series of culture regions before it came to be the "Chinese" culture region but, historically, China often has temporarily broken apart into separate culture regions in the past. This is always a latent tendency when the central government of China falters, as it did recently during the Cultural Revolution. However, in that the unique written language of China could always be universally used, in that religion never became a regionally centered culture trait, and in that important cultural mores spread far and wide, China has long been able to coalesce into one operating culture system when leadership exerted its influence sufficiently strongly. The regionalisms of China do not, essentially, provoke the inflammatory and militant responses that prevent cultural integration.

Laos, on the other hand, exists only on the political maps of the outside world, and its dilemmas involve questions of how to achieve the goals of an operating politico-cultural state in the first place, since these have never existed for the region now considered a political state by the outside world. Chiefly populated by a very diversified set of ethnic units whose cultural levels, technologic positions, and world views have no normative mean, unable to finance the basic institutions of an independent state, any group asserting its leadership faces an almost impossible set of problems. Currently beset by a struggle for spatial control by elements foreign to the region, and faced with acceptance of one or another system of societal-state operation desired by no native inhabitant, Laos remains a pawn in a world game. Laos is neither an effective regional entity upon which to build a state in spatial terms nor an operating state in the true sense, and it ought not have to be at this point. In a humane, peaceful, and dignified world Laos could remain a "world trusteeship" undergoing development toward the day when establishment of an independent spatial-cultural entity could assume its own responsibilities. In today's world such a status probably cannot obtain, but there is no certainty as to how or when some interim decision will place Laos into dependent status of some sort, thereby markedly altering its future regional development.

Korea for long periods of its early history was under divisive pressures from separate sources, from one of which sources (China) many of its cultural motivations were derived. For considerable periods of time Korea was then free of such pressures and was able to develop its cultural unity in its own way. Today, however, Korea finds itself again divided under pressures from without, roughly halved under two radically different politico-cultural systems, seemingly with little free initiative for an attempt at consolidation under conditions of free choice. Every year that passes increases the difficulties of reconciliation of the two segments. Within each segment there are internal pressures for continued development within the present framework. We may well be witnessing the splitting of a former regional entity into two units which never can coalesce in the future, and if the present divisions continue for more than a few years, this will most likely be the case. The dilemmas of the future now exist for both units rather than merely for one.

The problems for Taiwan are peculiar to its irrational political status in world groupings, but the problems for Taiwan in her own right are significant. Imbued with the sense of obligation to carry on the standard of traditional Chinese culture while modernizing in accommodation of today's world presents the leadership of Taiwan with a dual set of problems not equally share by all members of the island population. Taiwanese Chinese (those long resident on the island and descended from earlier immigrants) are not in full sympathy with the aims of mainland Chinese (those resident in Taiwan only since 1949 and after). Economically, Taiwan has been making real strides, but the other three phases of modern independent development face international pressures over which Taiwan cannot, possibly, exert exclusive control.

The Philippines started out her independence, in 1945, in high hopes of successfully achieving solutions to all four issues, but the record is spotty progress and incomplete success so far. Political status and control over spatial elements are not in question, but the problems of diversified economic development affecting all Filipinos have proved thorny indeed, and the island state has not been able to bring progress clearly within the grasp of the agrarian sector. This failure owes largely to the continuance of traditional economic-cultural institutionalisms that surround the agrarian peasantry with elements of bondage that no administrative leadership seems either able or willing to break. And as a traditional Roman Catholic country the problems of modernizing of a cultural identity and of taking the population problem in hand seem far from solution. Rather than coming toward a stable national cultural identity Filipinos seem to be moving in dichotomous fashion; "Juan de la Cruz" continues to follow his water buffalo in the muddy furrow of a rice field in the traditional agrarian scene while a modern day "Juan Tamad" (a legendary folk hero who achieves his end, no matter how) has become a sophisticated industrialist and a "big man" in city affairs, with a finger in political controls that keep Juan de la Cruz anchored in the rural backcountry. Government no longer seems to operate for all Filipinos despite the recent dictatorial takeover.

Indonesia continues a political state through no real efforts of her own, but the set of problems looms large and serious. Animosity toward the Dutch has worn thin as a *raison d'etre*, political indecision, financial instability, and internal insecurity have followed Soekarno, and economic indecision regarding production systems remains normative. In the face of tremendous agrarian pressures from a rural peasantry having far too little land on Java-Madura, domestic steps in advancing the national economy seem to rest on outside pressures for the development of Indonesian resources. Although *Bahasa Indonesia* is spreading as a national language, this is a slim basis for the evolution of a national cultural system, and since colonial days there has mushroomed a bureaucracy, largely devoid of leadership in the post-Soekarno era, that seems chiefly content to shuffle papers and draw its monthly rations. It may well be that the current period is one of latent activity, a holding period during which the populace makes up its mind about future directions and programs, for which the rest of the earth contributes best by displaying patience, but if this is the case then patience must be enduring. Ethnic diversity, regional variation by islands in folk culture systems, and separatist pulls by island subgroups still counter the efforts toward national cultural unity.

Malaysia essentially is a first-time new state with all the problems surrounding the first efforts to create a set of national cultural mores, but it is a state in which divergent ethnic groups must find a common denominator for cultural and political nationalism. The historic background is Malay and Islamic but only loosely so, and the integration of immigrant Chinese and Indians and the annexed Borneo near-Malay cultural systems into a new "Malaysianism" is uncertainly probing a path through the hindering communal animosities that regularly arise. A latent competitivism between Chinese and Malays, chiefly, expresses itself in an informal birth-rate competition, the use of economic *versus* political power, parallel but separate educational systems, preserved communal restrictions, and other selective communalisms that shackle the solid integration of all citizenry into a single national culturalism. Providing that the latent cultural communalisms can be held in check until a synthetic cultural nationalism can arise to support the now operative political nationalism, Malaysia can become a successful political state, but the growing pains still burst forth occasionally in periods of violence, and such will recur in the near future.

Culturally and psychologically Brunei should be a member of the Malaysian state, but since adherence would have deprived the Sultan of Brunei of his oil royalties in terms of personal income, he declined. In a peaceful world Brunei can continue separatist, on sufferance, to be blanketed into whatever general fate attends the success of Malaysia. Singapore, initially a member state of Malaysia, withdrew when it became clear that Malaysia would depreciate the role of Singapore as a world port. Going it alone since 1965, Singapore is seeking to play a role for Southeast Asia such as Hongkong plays to China. A Chinese city-state on an important sea-trade route, Singapore has turned to industrialization and complete modernization and is plugging her role as an efficient "central place" in the economic realm of Southeast Asia. If efficient leadership continues able to promote this perception by the world at large, Singapore may well succeed in its effort.

Thailand is the one southern state that never went through a period of colonialism, either in terms of training or "exploitation." A long-term cultural nationalism stands behind the Thai experience of taking over a separate region in the lowlands of Southeast Asia, and both serve as bases for the development of a modern regional state. The lack of a period of colonialism, however, promoted the continuance of a native system of culture, not thereby forcing the processes of cultural change as those took place in several other portions of the oriental world. The Thai have proven skillful at playing off outsiders, the better to preserve their independence and cultural integrity. Faced with the modern pressures for cultural change Thailand sometimes seems to lag in many ways, but there is clear evidence that the Thai are attempting to modernize their national system only at the rate at which they can control the changes in conformity with the basic aspects of Thai culture. It perhaps is too early to tell whether or not this will be completely successful. The border regions of Thailand contain small long-resident clusters of non-Thai ethnic groups toward which the Thai have not shown complete skill at integration, although so far these problems have been nuisances rather than significantly serious. Bangkok and its nearby towns contain a significant Chinese population neither politically restricted nor fully integrated into Thai cultural nationalism, this minority possibly provoking a more difficult problem. The near future constitutes a critical period in the determination of Thailand to control processes of modernization, for the rates of change are becoming more rapid and beset with more difficult issues. Providing that the Thai can take the more critical aspects of modernization in stride, Thailand could form one of the more successful modern states of the oriental world.

Cambodia has led a tenuous national existence since the sixteenth century and was saved political partition and cultural decimation in the late nineteenth century by the assumption of a French protectorate as part of the building of a French colonial holding. In a peaceful postwar Southeast Asia Cambodia could have slowly rebuilt its cultural and political strength, but recent events have taken a different turn. The temporary assertion of neutralism did not save Cambodia from sharing in the violence affecting the two Vietnams and Laos, and its future as a separate and independent state now seems open to question. Within a Communist realm, in the future, there would remain problems of the restoration of Cambodian cultural nationalism that probably would be somewhat greater than were the future to lie outside the Communist realm. The modernizing of the Cambodian culture system will take place sometime in the future, and there are sure to be severe problems of structuring a political state of stable proportions no matter under which political system the development takes place.

The Burmese did not fare well in the annexation of their region into the British Indian colonial administration, and they suffered severely at the hands of the Japanese during World War II. Burmese independence in 1948 saw the expulsion of all aliens and a gradual retreat from the world by the virtual closing of Burma to outside contact. The Burmans were the most numerous among the several ethnic stocks inhabiting the territory of political Burma, and the Burmans sought to make Burman ethnic culturalism into Burmese cultural nationalism with political control in the hands of the Burman Burmese. Militant reaction against Burman domination has characterized the whole political independence of Burma, after a period in which British colonial administration had maintained an unsteady pattern of truce between ethnic regional communities within Burma. Only slow and very diffident moves toward modernization have been taken in Burma, and a kind of Buddhist socialism that strikes occidentals as related to never-never land has been instituted as an integral component of the new politico-economic structure of the Burmese political state. The peoples of Burma have cared little for world status and do not view modernization, political efficiency, or economic growth valuable enough to be worth prejudicing independence. The Karen, Shan, Kachin, Palaung, and Chin regional minorities do not share effectively in the formulation of a future Burma, but whether or not a successful national cultural and political state can become operative without their inclusion in more than nominal terms is an open question. In legal terms Burma is a political state, but in the full sense of the term in the modern world Burma has not yet achieved a successful operating structure, and the indications are that this will take considerable more time in the future to achieve.

Ceylon, as a small island state with a long history of outside participation in and contribution to island life, finds itself a mixture of culturalisms that have not blended into one cultural nationalism. The political state operates above strong cultural communalisms by developing welfare economics into a pattern trying to provide for all in a way against which no communal sector could protest. Nationalizing of certain former private holdings and enterprises and the rejection of the former elite leadership have not succeeded in bringing the communities together, communities among which religion, language, social status, political privilege, and economic opportunity become militant issues. Uneasy truces, makeshift decisions, and temporizing over basic policy continue to be the rule, and basic problems in the operation of a single spatial entity continue to mount as the population increases. Sinhalese put store in their tradition as a leader of the Buddhist world, and in the role of Buddhism in Ceylon's life—items not shared by other ethnic groups. The pragmatic hard-decision issues continue to be avoided concerning the developing of an integrated national state, so that Ceylon faces an uncertain future in terms of progressive economic and cultural development. Aspects of instability will continue for the foreseeable future unless some magic inventiveness in cultural institutionalisms can be developed to bring the several Ceylonese cultures into one focus.

India, like China, is a grouping of regions that formerly held regional and local cultures. India never achieved the historic cultural unity that came in China, and provincialisms that are sometimes more sectionalisms and linguistic specialisms loom larger in India than they do in China. Separation of the former Indian cultural realm on the basis of religion in 1947, India being the Hindu zone, was more opportunist than realistic in many respects, but it produced a working boundary limit to the Indian state that could be more effectively demarcated at a later date. Those precise boundary problems remain and, though minor in the Thar Desert sector, they are not minor in Kashmir. India carries a very heavy weight of culturalisms out of the past, the modernizing of which is proving sorely troublesome. India has long carried a status as one of the superior states of the oriental world and, lacking the egocentric view held by the Chinese, the status position of the Indian state has been no real problem. For India the development of modern economic systems that provide adequately for all the structured social ranks has proven the foremost problem of modernization, a problem that is proving singularly recalcitrant. In a large society such as India the pressures for political policy directions are bound to be diverse, as they are proving to be, and India is being pressured toward a stronger from of socialism than is acceptable to many. For all the nonviolence of Indian culture, the pattern of feeling often boils over into militant and violent protest, and political violence is becoming more frequent and widespread. The problems of internal cultural-political-economic synthesis of the complexly structured Indian society remain serious ones that will bother India for some time to come, whatever basic form is taken in the future by the Indian political state.

The development of the spatially divided state of Pakistan, separated by a thousand miles of distance and by many aspects of culturalism, was against all odds at the beginning. By the late 1960's, it began to look as though perhaps the proposition might work, but events of late 1970–1971 have proven otherwise in rather tragic terms. Pakistan was an artificial state structured initially on the spatial plurality of the Islamic faith, but religion alone could not preserve real unity and build cultural strength in the face of unequal politico-economic administration of the two portions, with domination amounting almost to colonial control exerted by the western segment. Since there now are the two new states of Pakistan (former West Pakistan) and Bangladesh (former East Pakistan) replacing the two-part Pakistan, some of the cultural problems are simplified, but the economic and political problems replacing them constitute tremendous handicaps, and ultimate solutions are nowhere in sight at this writing.

The case of Japan has been left to the last since Japan has been noted as an exception to the rule in several chapters. One might choose to say that Japan has no obvious problems in the modern world, as these have been itemized in paragraphs above. Japan has a strong political structure, a thriving economy that has removed the agrarian sector almost entirely from the position of rural peasantry, and a strong national identity in both political and cultural terms. Japan, however, has never occupied the position of a world leader in clearly evident terms, needing thereby to temper her "public relations" approach to other cultures. The aggressiveness that has characterized the modernizing of Japan often rubs the wrong way in intercultural dealings, and Japan will have some of the problems in the future that go with any position of great strength and power. The Japanese now are becoming aware of this and are beginning to think through their position in the world at large.

There remain only bits and pieces in this thumbnail coverage of the dilemmas present in the oriental world. Nepal and Bhutan occupy positions between the two spatial giants, India and China, and their political regionalisms are subject not only to pressures but also to tolerances of both. Cultural and economic problems for modern political states are but barely coming into focus. In a tolerant world these can be worked out in the future, but tolerance and helpfulness must come from both sides, for their landlocked positions give them little freedom. For all intents and purposes Sikkim, a princely state between Bhutan on the east and Nepal on the west, fit under the Indian rubric. So do the Maldives, a series of coral islands off the southwest coast of India. The sole remaining Portuguese holding in the East Indies, Portuguese Timor, is a backwater unit now that the sandalwood trade has declined, and it continues on sufferance to live its quiet and simple rural life. Were it worth any trouble Indonesia could take it over with but little change in the tenor of things. Hongkong continues its tenor of life too, but it is too valuable as a busy mart of international trade for China to upset at this point. At a later point, when China's position in the international community has been rectified adequately, the Chinese may end the lease on the New Territories and request the cession of Hongkong Island. Hongkong has less of a "we British" air about it than formerly, but it remains close to unique in its internationalness and will so remain for the near future. Historically, the Ryukyu Islands held a minor position as an autonomous unit within the cultural mosaic of the oriental world. The very size, population, and cultural strength of this island culture was not sufficient to carry it forward into the modern world in autonomous position. Attached to Japan through no will of its own, and temporarily detached after World War II, the Ryukyu Islands are in process of returning to provincial position within the Japanese state structure. Culturally oriented toward Japan for some time past, this may well be better than trying to go it alone in the modern world.

The above expression of dilemmas and problems brings to mind the questions of how modernization will go and what routes it may take in the several parts of the oriental world. There should stand out the impressions that all the regional cultural units are seeking to accommodate themselves to the pressures of modern political nationalism and modern economic development, at particular prices in particular ways. Between Burma and Japan there is evidently a strong gap in the will to face the issues. In good part it is this will to face the issues that marks the degree of success in each national society, although in several cases the pressures of the outside world are being exerted in such a way that the eventual solutions are complicated and involve much more than the simple willingness to tackle cultural problems.

Commentary in Conclusion

Rather than make this small volume on a very large subject into a cryptic encyclopedia carrying one-sentence pronouncements on all salient geographic phenomena, I have dealt in a few thematic discussions of critically significant phases of the geography of the oriental world. The overriding concern has been to contribute to an understanding of why and how the modern oriental world seems to be a troubled realm and how the several regional entities stand as parts of that oriental world. In presenting essays on critically significant themes many important geographic problems have not found place, and this study in no way constitutes a full-scale geographic treatise. The essays are exemplary and the text has not been burdened with specific place or country reference in regard to every thematic discussion. The simple "geographic facts" held to be so important to some in geography have been paid scant heed throughout these essays, but several series of data are presented in tabular form at the end of this chapter which may serve those who put stock in such facts (Table 1, through 5).

One of the themes of this study has been the disposition of physical environments in such a way that the southeastern quadrant of the Eurasian continent provided a goodly number of regional cells into which early and underdeveloped culture groups could move, there to find surroundings in which each could formulate particular variants of culture systems. In some cases these environments were single cells spaced out in such ways as to facilitate occupancy by a single culture group, but in other cases clusters of regional cells were arranged in linked patterns in very large physical regions in such a way as to make possible the historical accrual of related culture systems whose basic components were shared by all the culture groups resident in the cluster. If this schematic theme seems worked overly hard, and aspects of its geomorphic determinism seem strongly put, this is but a spatial convenience and not meant to assert that this is the way the politico-cultural structure of a part of the oriental world had to come out. After all, culture groups did not have to continue to occupy those particular regional cells, but groups were free to move where they chose. The China cluster of regional cells clearly demonstrates this, for some groups chose to remain in the China cluster, but others chose to leave in search of new regional environments. Some of the groups choosing to remain in China still are not fully engulfed within the enveloping folds of Chinese culture, for they constitute cultural minorities now given territorial status within the Chinese politico-cultural state. The Thai could have elected to remain in China to fight it out (militarily, politically, and culturally), but they elected to emigrate from China, in the end finding a regional cell in which they could develop a regional culture system on their own terms. But no reader should find in these thematic essays the fictional label of cultural determinism either in the suggestion that the subcontinent of China Proper (plus Manchuria in the modern era) houses just one large culture system because the Chinese have been better able to override the physical geography of the zone in more effective terms than were the European culture groups able to override the physical geography of the subcontinent of Europe. The Chinese have not always been able to override that physical geography, for at times in history there have been from three to eight "China's" as the cluster of regions reverted to its physical regionalism (the historian conventionally has elected only one regional entity, normally, by which to keep his chronology continuous and his dynastic systemization intact).

In the broad overview the oriental world can be seen as a bipolar world in which two separate culture systems stand at the margins, those of China and India. It is evident that these two culture systems provided the accepted motivations for some of the other regional culture systems of the oriental world, Korea, Japan, and Vietnam following the Chinese system, and Ceylon and Sumatra-Java following the Indian system. But it is notable that some peoples rejected either outright acceptance of either system or assimilation into the matrix of the two culture systems. Thus the "midlatitudes" between the "poles" show the growth of the selective but mixed assemblages of elements into the culture systems of the Southeast Asia shatter belt. Early India reached out more than did China to implant abroad the aspects of Indian culture, as far east as Java-Bali-Lombok. From the too close position against Chinese culture many early culture groups migrated southward into the terminal corners and island fringes of the Eurasian continent in order to escape conversion into Chinese. In more modern time both Indians and Chinese have themselves migrated into the shatter-belt zone, normally carrying important aspects of their culture with them, to further complicate the socio-cultural structure of the shatter belt. Both "polar" cultures have long looked at the shatter-belt zone with a participative concern in an overlapping but never directly competitive manner.

Both polar cultures, of course, have been subjected to influences from outside the oriental world in terms of cultural diffusion, militant land contact, and migrational trends into the two regional poles. Both have absorbed from the midlatitudes what the Chinese term "barbarian" traits and culture complexes. Most of the militant migrational elements from outside the oriental world (southwest Asia or central Asia) became absorbed into either Indian or Chinese culture, whereas the adoption of barbarian traits from the midlatitudes, in both directions, has served to broaden the two culture systems and to provide for greater similarity throughout the whole of the oriental world. Historically, the influences from outside the oriental world chiefly became spent in the polar sectors, and only by cultural diffusionary processes did alien influences reach the midlatitudes.

In strong contrast to the ancient pattern, occidental cultural intrusion into the oriental world approached that world from a different compass bearing, from out of the west, and by sea. The easterly course of this new influence in time skirted the whole of the coastal fringe, penetrating inland in variable manner after the establishment of landfall port bases. Thus, the midlatitudes became affected directly by new cultural influences unprotected by the shield formerly provided by the polar cultures. The new influences came at a time when much of the oriental world was in religious, cultural, and political flux, when strange new patterns could be quite disruptive. And disruptive the occidental influences have proven to be, in almost every aspect of the traditional cultures of the oriential world. The era of political colonialism is almost always viewed as a retrogressive, exploitive, domineering, and costly affair. That it was in many ways, and no counter argument has been presented here. At the same time, however, the era served as a training period for those societies that went through the colonial experience. And how shall we view many of the complexes of culture that came with the occidental intrusion? For example, the public health system was held a boon to mankind for the lives it saved, but do we now turn around and fault the Occident for its introduction into the oriental world now that population growth has become stifling? For good or for bad, the occidental intrusion into the oriental culture world set off many series of complex changes in culture systems, changes that have not run their courses to terminal cultural developments.

Throughout the oriental world the variety of reaction has been great and far reaching. Many societies find the complexity of the present all too troublesome and cast the blame for their present fates upon the Occident. One or two societies appear diffident in the face of the modern world at large. One or two have vigorously grasped the "tools" of the modern world and compete with that whole modern world on its own terms. One cannot extract averages, means, standard deviations, and other such from the total performances of the several members of the oriental world, but it clearly is evident that the processes of cultural change still have far to go before any large sector of cultural change can be said to have arrived at a level of stability.

Lastly, it is clear that culture groups have matured to a considerable degree in that the politico-cultural map of the oriental world remains framed around the patterns of regions which have long given it identity. For all that the present politico-cultural structure of Burma or Vietnam is somewhat unstable and suffering the throes of change, it is clear that those separate culture groups that could find physical environments that were conducive to evolutionary development have matured into regional culture systems possessing such integrity and lasting strength as to continue to hold a place on the map within the heart areas of the chosen physical environments. Lowland Burma still is the core of a regional culture, as is southern Japan, and the island of Java. For all that the spectrum of political stability and cultural cohesiveness shows a wide range of color indicating variable success in surmounting the problems of cultural change in the last millennium, the regional identities remain about what they were, in broad terms. All of which suggests that after the several regional members of the oriental world have suffered through the trials of culture change in the modern era the "map" of their distributions will not have changed much as those regional cultures find mature expression. Patience upon the part of the rest of the earth is called for while the complex processes of culture change run their courses.

TABLE 1. Data and Estimates Concerning Population as of 1970[a]

Country	Square miles	Population '000	Projected pop. 1980 '000	Birth rate per 1,000	Death rate per 1,000	Share urbanized %	Capital and population in '000	
Bangladesh	55,126	72,000	98,000	52	27	8	Dacca	600
Bhutan	19,305	1,100	1,230	*	*	3	Thimpu	12
Brunei	2,226	135,600	180,000	43.9	6.4	30	Bandar Seri Bagawan	36
Burma	261,789	28,400	37,600	40.3	19	11	Rangoon	1,400
Cambodia	69,898	6,800	10,700	41	20	16	Pnom Penh	500
Ceylon	25,532	13,200	16,300	32	7.9	17	Colombo	800
China	3,690,546	760,000	863,000	33	14	20	Peking	7,350
Hongkong	356	4,100	4,600	18.9	5.8	†	Victoria	†
India	1,269,640	547,367	687,000	42.8	16	21	Delhi	4,100
Indonesia	735,268	124,200	174,000	42	21	16	Djakarta	4,542
Japan	142,767	103,900	113,000	18.3	6.7	60	Tokyo	11,800
Korea, North	46,540	13,800	17,400	40.5	12.8	25	Pyongyang	650
Korea, South	38,012	32,500	52,140	38	12.0	32	Seoul	4,100
Laos	91,429	3,050	3,700	42	20	8	Ventiane	140
Macao	006	280	310	*	*	†	Macao	†
Malaysia	128,430	12,000	14,400	38	7.6	33	Kuala Lumpur	462
Maldives	115	115	126	50.2	22	12	Malé	14
Nepal	54,362	11,120	13,600	41	24	7	Kathmandu	333
Pakistan	310,403	60,700	83,000	50	26	24	Islamabad	50
Philippines	115,826	39,319	52,000	50	13.6	32	Quezon City	545
Sikkim	2,745	194	245	*	*	13	Gangtok	18
Singapore	224	2,110	2,536	22.1	5.2	†	Singapore	†
Taiwan	13,885	14,875	16,375	29.3	5.5	30	Taipei	1,818
Thailand	200,148	35,700	52,600	38	8.1	10	Bangkok	2,100
Timor	7,383	585	800	*	*	13	Dili	56
Vietnam, North	63,360	21,000	27,800	*	*	*	Hanoi	500
Vietnam, South	66,263	18,500	21,300	37	16.2	*	Saigon	1,800

[a] In some cases data are from 1969.
* Data inadequate or not available.
† Data not relevant to this item.
Sources: *Far Eastern Economic Review*, United Nations, and country handbooks.

TABLE 2. Selected Agricultural and Economic Data as of 1970[a]

Country	Land in producing farms '000,000 ac.	Reserve farmland '000,000 ac.	Population density per s/m	Agricul. density per s/m	Economic aid, US$ 1967–1969 ave.'000,000	Import 1970, US$ '000,000	Exports 1970, US$ '000,000
Bangladesh	22.5	1.1	1,306	1,987	*	*	*
Bhutan	1.0	.500	44	*	.340	*	*
Brunei	.073	.500	61	*			
Burma	22.8	4.6	108	797	20	144	105
Cambodia	5.1	4.8	90	850	12	3	3.1
Ceylon	4.3	2.3	517	1,964	46	389	340
China	295	*	206	1,590	b	1,586	1,580
Hongkong	.03	†	11,182	†	.630	2,905	2,514
India	350	46	431	1,000	1,072	2,130	1,957
Indonesia	44.0	10.5	168	1,806	300	880	1,009
Japan	14.25	.300	721	4,666	b	18,881	19,318
Korea, North	5.4	.800	292	1,635		*	
Korea, South	5.8	.400	825	3,586	314	1,983	828
Laos	2.5	3.5	33	*	67	42.2	2.1
Macao	†	†	46,666	†	*	*	*
Malaysia	7.5	4.1	93	1,175	50	1,389	1,680
Maldives	*	*	1,000	*	.210	*	*
Nepal	4.2	2.8	204	1,694	6	*	*
Pakistan	47.6	30.0	192	816	467	1,090	1,061
Philippines	22.6	10.2	338	1,113	117	*	*
Sikkim	*	*	66	†	*	*	*
Singapore	.03	0	931	4,140	11	2,464	1,554
Taiwan	2.3	.600	1,050	872	71	1,560	1,524
Thailand	26.2	6.8	178	468	73	1,253	697
Timor	.800	*	79	*	*	*	*
Vietnam, North	7.5	.800	331	*	*	*	*
Vietnam, South	9.3	4.7	276	*	453	550	11

a In some cases data are from 1969.
b Contributor nation.
* Data inadequate or not available.

† Data not relevant to this item.

Sources: *Far Eastern Economic Review*, United Nations, and country handbooks.

TABLE 3. Data on Primary Food Crop Staples as of 1970[a]

Country	Rice production '000 tons	Maize production '000 tons	Wheat production '000 tons	Sweet potatoes production '000 tons	Peanuts production '000 tons	Sugar production[b] '000 tons	Copra production '000 tons
Bangladesh	11,800	20	80	275	35	200	*
Bhutan	†	†	†	†	*	0	0
Brunei	4.6	0.5	0	1.5	*	*	*
Burma	8,023	150	73	*	521	90	*
Cambodia	2,732	121	0	19	23	†	1.6
Ceylon	1,475	10	0	60	7	11	210
China	94,000	23,000	27,000	80,000	3,000	3,100	c
Hongkong	18	0	0	7	0	0	0
India	69,600	6,500	24,540	1,650	6,400	4,402	280
Indonesia	23,064	2,888	0	3,029	293	1,017	1,281
Japan	12,689	51	474	2,564	130	430	0
Korea, North	2,500	1,800	85	250	8	*	0
Korea, South	4,439	67	356	1,200	15	*	0
Laos	700	25	*	5	2	*	0
Macao	0	0	0	0	0	0	0
Malaysia	1,400	10	0	65	4	*	140
Maldives	0	0	0	0	0	0	10
Nepal	2,350	900	242	*	*	16	0
Pakistan	2,400	650	7,400	300	111	451	*
Philippines	5,234	2,008	0	1,100	17	1,926	1,656
Sikkim	15	38	3	2	*	*	0
Singapore	0	0	0	4	0	0	*
Taiwan	2,462	57	10	3,700	122	734	*
Thailand	13,400	1,950	*	260	22	460	130
Timor	14	18	0	8	*	*	2.5
Vietnam, North	4,200	25	*	900	46	†	0
Vietnam, South	5,600	31.6	0	230	32.6	†	*

a In some cases data are from 1969.
b For China and Japan production includes beet sugar; elsewhere reference is to cane sugar.
c Now under production in Hainan and coastal Kwangtung, but data not available on production.
* Data inadequate or not available.
† Crop plant common in domestic use, the data lacking concerning commercial production.
Sources: *Far Eastern Economic Review*, United Nations, and country handbooks.

TABLE 4. Selected Secondary Crop Patterns as of 1970[a]

Country	Coffee production '000 tons	Tea production '000 tons	Tobacco production '000 tons	Pepper production '000 tons	Cotton production '000 tons	Jute production '000 tons	Rubber production '000 tons
Bangladesh	0	34.4	61	*	2	1,490	0
Bhutan	0	*	†	0	0	0	0
Brunei	*	0	†	2.0	0	0	0.300
Burma	0.600	†	54	1.8	42	28	14
Cambodia	0.600	*	9.7	1.6	6.0	9.3	46
Ceylon	†	238	7.0	11.1	†	*	164
China	†	417	760	0	2,100	0	0
Hongkong	0	0	†	0	0	0	0
India	63.5	405	338	34	2,800	1,170	80
Indonesia	159	81	59	23	†	*	779
Japan	0	91	150	0	0	0	0
Korea, North	0	0	40	0	†	0	0
Korea, South	0	0	76.5	0	†	0	*
Laos	3.0	2	3.8	*	2.1	0	0
Macao	0	0	0	0	0	0	0
Malaysia	60	3	3.0	31.5	0	*	1,275
Maldives	0	0	0	0	0	0	0
Nepal	*	*	7.0	*	*	53	0
Pakistan	*	0	210	0	529	0	0
Philippines	47	0	61	0	5.0	2.1	24.0
Sikkim	*	8.6	*	†	0	*	0
Singapore	†	0	0.5	0	0	0	2.0
Taiwan	†	27	20	0	†	13	0
Thailand	*	1.5	93	4.5	52	210	300
Timor	5.0	*	*	*	*	*	44
Vietnam, North	10	2.8	4.0	*	†	†	0
Vietnam, South	35	8.1	8.3	*	0.200	6.0	27.5

[a] In some cases data are from 1969.

* Data inadequate or not available.

† Crop plant present and product used at home, but no known commercial production.

Sources: *Far Eastern Economic Review*, United Nations, and country handbooks.

TABLE 5. Selected Important Animal Populations as of 1970[a]

Country	Pigs in '000's	Cattle in '000's	Water buffalo in '000's	Sheep in '000's	Goats in '000's	Horses in '000's
Bangladesh	†	6,000	6,000	*	7,000	*
Bhutan	b	b	b	b	b	b
Brunei	10	†	16	0	†	†
Burma	1,300	6,750	1,000	210	700	38
Cambodia	1,078	1,415	400	†	†	8
Ceylon	124	1,225	850	29	500	†
China	213,000	74,000	16,000	24,000	60,000	7,000
Hongkong	390	13	1.0	0	†	†
India	4,890	175,000	53,000	41,000	64,000	2,000
Indonesia	2,667	700	3,816,000	2,450	600	620
Japan	6,535	4,155	0	800	190	300
Korea, North	1,280	700	0	18	170	25
Korea, South	1,398	1,255	0	2.3	109	18
Laos	1,000	39	900	35	*	20
Macao	96		0	0	2	0
Malaysia	605	310	300	0	320	†
Maldives	†	0	0	†	0	0
Nepal	200	2,930	3,000	2,100	2,300	†
Pakistan	†	38,000	10,000	12,000	11,050	500
Philippines	6,250	1,644	3,600	40	700	300
Sikkim	*	b	*	*	b	*
Singapore	402	7	4	0	2	0
Taiwan	4,000	104	300	†	160	†
Thailand	4,300	5,200	7,000	40	35	200
Timor	216	59	110	34	217	100
Vietnam, North	6,200	865	1,830	†	*	50
Vietnam, South	3,553	1,033	625	†	44	10

[a] In some cases data are from 1969.
[b] Animal is significant to local economy, but data on numbers lacking.
* Data inadequate or not available.
† Animal present in small numbers but not generally kept.

Sources: *Far Eastern Economic Review*, United Nations, and country handbooks.

selected bibliography

The Journal of Asian Studies publishes an annual supplement that contains bibliographies of books and articles on all of southern and eastern Asia, with coverage in the social sciences, humanities, art, and linguistics. *Current Geographical Publications* covers the subject of geography somewhat selectively.

AHMAD, KAZI, S., *A Geography of Pakistan*, 2nd ed. Karachi: Oxford University Press, 1964.

BUCHANAN, KEITH, *The Southeast Asian World, An Introductory Essay*. London: G. Bell and Sons, 1967.

——, *The Transformation of the Chinese Earth*. New York: Praeger, 1970.

CHANG, CHI-WEN (ed.), *Rural Asia Marches Forward, Focus on Agricultural and Rural Development*. Laguna, Philippines: UPCA Textbook Board, 1969.

COEDES, G., *The Making of Southeast Asia*. Berkeley and Los Angeles: University of California Press, 1966.

——, *The Indianized States of Southeast Asia*, 3rd ed. Honolulu: East-West Center Press, 1968.

DEMPSTER, PRUE, *Japan Advances, a Geographical Study*. London: Methuen, 1967.

FRYER, DONALD W., *Emerging Southeast Asia, A Study in Growth and Stagnation*. London: George Philip and Son, 1970.

Far Eastern Economic Review, Yearbook. Hongkong: Far Eastern Economic Review, annual publication.

HALL, D. G. E., *Atlas of Southeast Asia*. London: Methuen, 1964.

HAMMER, E., *Vietnam Yesterday and Today*. New York: Holt, 1966.

HERMANN, A., *An Historical Atlas of China*. Chicago: Aldine, 1966.

HSIEH, CHIAO-MIN, *Taiwan—ilha Formosa, a Geography in Perspective*. Washington, D. C.: Butterworths, 1964.

JACKSON, JAMES C., *Sarawak, A Geographical Survey of a Developing State*. London: University of London Press, 1968.

KARAN, P. P., and W. M. JENKINS, *Nepal, A Cultural and Physical Geography*. Lexington: University of Kentucky Press, 1963.

LEE, YONG-LENG, *North Borneo (Sabah), A Study in Settlement Geography*. Singapore: Eastern Universities Press, 1965.

LEE, YONG-LENG, *Population and Settlement in Sarawak*. Singapore: Asia Pacific Press, 1970.

MCCUNE, S., *Korea, Land of Broken Calm*. New York: Van Nostrand Reinhold, 1966.

MCVEY, RUTH T., *Indonesia*. New Haven: Yale University SoutheastAsia Studies, 1963.

von der Mehden, Fred, *Religion and Nationalism in Southeast Asia, Burma, Indonesia, Philippines*. Madison: University of Wisconsin Press, 1963.

NASH, MANNING, *The Golden Road to Modernity, Village Life in Contemporary Burma*. New York: Wiley, 1965.

NELSON, RAYMOND, *The Philippines*. New York: Walker, 1968.

NITISASTRO, WIDJOJO, *Population Trends in Indonesia*. Ithaca: Cornell University Press, 1970.

OOI JIN-BEE, *Land, People, and Economy in Malaya*. London: Longmans, 1963.

PEDELABORDE, P., *The Monsoon*. London: Methuen, 1963.

PENDLETON, R. L., *Thailand, Aspects of Land and Life*. New York: Duell, Sloan and Pierce, 1962.

PERKINS, DWIGHT H., *Agricultural Development in China, 1368–1968*. Chicago: Aldine, 1969.

ROMEIN, JAN, *The Asian Century, A History of Modern Nationalism in Asia*. Berkeley and Los Angeles: University of California Press, 1962.

SHAND, R. T. (ed.), *Agricultural Development in Asia*. Berkeley and Los Angeles: University of California Press, 1969.

SILCOCK, T. H., *The Economic Development of Thai Agriculture*. Ithaca: Cornell University Press, 1970.

SIMKIM, C. G. F., *The Traditional Trade of Asia*. London: Oxford University Press, 1968.

SPENCER, J. E., *Shifting Cultivation in Southeastern Asia*, Vol. 19. Berkeley and Los Angeles: University of California Publications in Geography, 1966.

————, and WILLIAM L. THOMAS, *Asia, East by South, A Cultural Geography*. New York: Wiley, 1971.

SPATE, O. H. K., and A. T. A. LEARMOUTH, *India and Pakistan, A General and Regional Geography*, 3rd ed. London: Methuen, 1967.

TAYYEB, A. *Pakistan, A Political Geography*. London: Oxford University Press, 1966.

TILMAN, R. O. (ed.), *Man, State, and Society in Contemporary Southeast Asia*. New York: Praeger, 1969.

TRAGER, F. H., *Burma from Kingdom to Republic*. New York: Praeger, 1966.

TREGEAR, T. R., *A Geography of China*. London: University of London Press, 1965.

TREWARTHA, GLENN T., *Japan, a Geography*. Madison: University of Wisconsin Press, 1965.

TUAN, YI-FU, *China*. Chicago: Aldine, 1969.

WERNSTEDT, F. L., and J. E. SPENCER, *Philippine Island World, a Physical Cultural and Regional Geography*. Berkeley and Los Angeles: University of California Press, 1967.

WILBER, DONALD NEWTON, *The Nations of Asia*. New York: Hart, 1966.

WILLMOTT, W. E., *The Chinese in Cambodia*. Vancouver: University of British Columbia, 1967.

WINT, GUY, *Asia Handbook*. London: Penguin, 1969.

Index

References to maps are printed in italics.

Agrarian expansion, maximum limit of, 61–62
Agrarian reform, futility of, 113–16
Agrarian systems:
  change in, after A.D. 1500, 92–96
  nature of oriental, 60
  variations in, 68–86
Agriculture:
  changes in, after A.D. 1500, 92–93
  commercial, growing trend in, 84–86
  impact of the Occident on, 82
  lands open to the modernization of, 118
  peasant gardening, 73–80
  plantation, 80–84
  problems in reforming, 113–16
  shifting cultivation, 69–72
  smallholder, 84–86
  variations in, 68–86
Animal life, zonation of, 15–18
Architecture, monumental, 43

Bangladesh, dilemmas facing, 130
Bhutan, 5, 130
Biogeographical criteria, 16
Brunei, dilemmas facing, 127
Burma:
  dilemmas facing, 128–29

nationalization of farmland in, 96
peoples of, 51

Cambodia:
  dilemmas facing, 128
  peoples of, 51
Capital formation, problems of, 116–17
Cashew nut tree, in India, 93–94
Caucasoid ethnic stocks, distribution of, 49
Ceylon:
  dilemmas facing, 129
  peoples of, 53–55
China:
  dilemmas facing, 123–25
  early agricultural systems, 73–74
  formulation of early culture system in, 87–88
  modernization of transport in, 95
  overpopulation of, 61
  peoples of, 53
  physical pattern of, 8
  regional landscapes of, 42
  revolutionary culture change in, 107
  as series of regional environments, 31
  soil maintenance systems in, 19
  structure of society in, 53